ALL LEARNING IS

SOCIAL AND

EMOTIONAL

ASCD MEMBER BOOK

Many ASCD members received this book as a
member benefit upon its initial release.

Learn more at: **www.ascd.org/memberbooks**

ALL LEARNING IS
SOCIAL AND EMOTIONAL

Helping Students Develop Essential Skills
for the Classroom and Beyond

NANCY FREY | DOUGLAS FISHER | DOMINIQUE SMITH

Alexandria, Virginia USA

1703 N. Beauregard St. • Alexandria, VA 22311-1714 USA
Phone: 800-933-2723 or 703-578-9600 • Fax: 703-575-5400
Website: www.ascd.org • E-mail: member@ascd.org
Author guidelines: www.ascd.org/write

Deborah S. Delisle, *Executive Director*; Stefani Roth, *Publisher*; Genny Ostertag, *Director, Content Acquisition*; Julie Houtz, *Director, Book Editing & Production*; Katie Martin, *Editor*; Judi Connelly, *Associate Art Director*; Melissa Johnston, *Graphic Designer*; Mike Kalyan, *Director, Production Services*; Keith Demmons, *Production Designer*; Trinay Blake, *E-Publishing Specialist*

All web links in this book are correct as of the publication date below but may have become inactive or otherwise modified since that time. If you notice a deactivated or changed link, please e-mail books@ascd.org with the words "Link Update" in the subject line. In your message, please specify the web link, the book title, and the page number on which the link appears.

PAPERBACK ISBN: 978-1-4166-2707-4   ASCD product #119033
PDF E-BOOK ISBN: 978-1-4166-2739-5; see Books in Print for other formats.
Quantity discounts are available: e-mail programteam@ascd.org or call 800-933-2723, ext. 5773, or 703-575-5773. For desk copies, go to www.ascd.org/deskcopy.

ASCD Member Book No. FY19-4 (Jan 2019 PSI+). ASCD Member Books mail to Premium (P), Select (S), and Institutional Plus (I+) members on this schedule: Jan, PSI+; Feb, P; Apr, PSI+; May, P; Jul, PSI+; Aug, P; Sep, PSI+; Nov, PSI+; Dec, P. For current details on membership, see www.ascd.org/membership.

Library of Congress Cataloging-in-Publication Data

Names: Frey, Nancy, 1959- author. | Fisher, Douglas, 1965- author. | Smith, Dominique, author.
Title: All learning is social and emotional : helping students develop essential skills for the classroom and beyond / Nancy Frey, Douglas Fisher, Dominique Smith.
Description: Alexandria, Virginia, USA : ASCD, [2019] | Includes bibliographical references and index.
Identifiers: LCCN 2018045145 (print) | LCCN 2018057509 (ebook) | ISBN 9781416627395 (PDF) | ISBN 9781416627074 (pbk.)
Subjects: LCSH: Affective education. | Social learning. | Learning, Psychology of.
Classification: LCC LB1072 (ebook) | LCC LB1072 .F74 2019 (print) | DDC 370.15/34--dc23
LC record available at https://lccn.loc.gov/2018045145

ALL LEARNING IS
SOCIAL AND EMOTIONAL

Helping Students Develop Essential Skills for the Classroom and Beyond

CHAPTER 1

Learning That's Worthwhile

Learning. That's what school is about, right? Regardless of our role in the education system, we all care that students learn. And we spend countless hours trying to ensure that students *do* learn. But exactly *what* students are expected to learn in school has been debated for decades. What should we teach? What do students need to learn and be able to do?

In many circles, the answer is simple. Schools need to teach, and students need to master, the core academic subjects. After all, most accountability measures focus on English and mathematics and sometimes science and social studies. For schools to be "successful" in ratings and rankings, their students must perform well on academic measures of achievement. In these schools, every instructional minute is meant to focus on academic skill development.

In other circles, "worthwhile learning" is expanded to include vocational and workplace skills. For example, the Secretary's Commission on Achieving Necessary Skills (SCANS, 1992) focused on one aspect of schooling they felt was missing: what they called the "learning a living" system. In addition to calling for basic skills such as literacy and numeracy, the SCANS report advocates focusing on the thinking skills necessary to put knowledge to work and the personal qualities that make workers dedicated and trustworthy.

Recognition and prioritization of skills that will be valuable in the workplace reflects a growing understanding that schools can influence more than just students' academic content knowledge. For example, California now includes "career pathways" as one of several ways students can demonstrate college and career readiness. In the new California accountability model, high school students must complete 300 hours of career and technical education coursework over three years to be considered "well prepared." Embedded in these courses are noncognitive skills such as working collaboratively with others to resolve problems, generating new products, communicating clearly, and making decisions with integrity. In other words, dispositions undergird the technical skills. These dispositions are aligned with industry competency skills outlined by the U.S. Department of Labor (SCANS, 1992).

In still other circles, worthwhile learning is understood to include mastery of social and emotional skills in additional to academic ones. Proponents of this wider view of learning—and obviously, we are among them—believe explicit instruction focused on the social and emotional aspects of learning (SEL) will result in improved academic learning.

To date, there have been limited efforts to address SEL in school accountability systems. In our home state of California, for example, suspension and expulsion rates are included in the multiple measures of school success. Some critics have argued that this encourages a too-permissive environment, where teachers and administrators are "soft on crime." Advocates counter that the ability to keep students in school is not just a valid *measure* of school success—it's an effective means of *increasing* it. In order to reduce suspensions and expulsions, schools must help students develop the social and emotional skills that will allow them to engage positively with one another, with their teachers, and with their learning.

A Closer Look at Social and Emotional Learning

SEL has been defined in a number of ways (see Humphrey et al., 2011). In general, it focuses on a set of social, emotional, behavioral, and character skills that support success in school, the workplace, relationships, and the community.

Although these skills affect academic learning, they are often considered "soft skills" or personal attributes rather than explicit targets of instruction. In fact, however, we are teaching SEL even if we don't think we are doing so. As Berman, Chaffee, and Sarmiento (2018) note, "How we teach is as instructive as *what* we teach. Just as the culture of the classroom must reflect social belonging and emotional safety, so can academic instruction embody and enhance these competencies and be enhanced by them" (p. 13). Teachers communicate these values every time they step in front of a class.

Current efforts to address the social and emotional needs of students can be traced to the work of Waters and Sroufe (1983), who describe competence as the ability "to generate and coordinate flexible, adaptive responses to demands and to generate and capitalize on opportunities in the environment" (p. 80). In other words, competent people are adaptive, they respond to situations in appropriate ways, and they seek opportunities in their communities. Isn't that what we want our students to be able to do? Accordingly, it seems that schools should be invested in developing this type of skill set in students.

The thinking about SEL has evolved over the years. In 1997, Elias and colleagues suggested that SEL comprises a set of competencies, which Durlak, Weissberg, Dymnicki, Taylor, and Schellinger (2011) further described as the ability to

- Recognize and manage emotions
- Set and achieve positive goals
- Appreciate the perspectives of others
- Establish and maintain positive relationships
- Make responsible decisions
- Handle interpersonal situations constructively (p. 406)

A few years later, the Collaborative for Academic, Social, and Emotional Learning (CASEL, 2005) identified five interrelated cognitive, affective, and behavioral competencies:

- *Self-awareness*—the capacity to reflect on one's own feelings, values, and behaviors.
- *Social awareness*—the ability to view situations from another perspective, respect the social and cultural norms of others, and celebrate diversity.

- *Relationship skills*—the ability to initiate and sustain positive connections with peers, teachers, families, and other groups.
- *Self-management*—the set of skills that includes self-motivation, goal setting, personal organization, self-discipline, impulse control, and use of strategies for coping with stress.
- *Responsible decision making*—the ability to make choices that consider the well-being of oneself and others.

Most recent to this publication, the Wallace Foundation model (see Jones, Bailey, Brush, & Kahn, 2018) identified three domains of SEL:

- *Cognitive regulation*—attention control, inhibitory control, working memory and planning, and cognitive flexibility.
- *Emotional processes*—emotion knowledge and expression, emotion and behavior regulation, and empathy or perspective taking.
- *Social/interpersonal skills*—understanding social cues, conflict resolution, and prosocial behavior.

Does SEL Belong in Schools?

Speaking of the Wallace Foundation, its work is guided by the principle "Say more only when you know more." In *All Learning Is Social and Emotional*, we have taken this advice to heart. Anyone who carefully follows the research on social and emotional learning is wise to avoid making too many definitive claims about its effect. However, one thing we *do* believe definitively is that classroom learning always includes cognitive, social, and emotional aspects.

As teachers, administrators, and consultants, we have worked with thousands of students and teachers over the years. We have worked across the general, special, and vocational curriculum in elementary, middle, and high schools, and in nearly every configuration of schooling. Based on these experiences and on our review of the research, we have concluded that because teachers unquestionably influence students' social and emotional development, they have a responsibility to do so in a way that is positive and deliberate.

As we described in the previous section, there are a number of ways to frame thinking about the social and emotional learning needs of students, and there have been hundreds of programs developed to support the effective development of social and emotional skills. Alongside the development of various approaches to SEL, there have been concurrent concerns about how best to formally integrate this aspect of learning into educators' work.

It makes sense to address three common questions about SEL before we go any farther.

Does Focusing on SEL Take Away from Academics?

It is true that there are only so many minutes that teachers get with students and that maximizing learning during those minutes is critical. Research suggests that time spent on SEL can facilitate academic learning (e.g., Durlak et al., 2011; Hawkins, Smith, & Catalano, 2004). As Jones and colleagues (2018) explain, "Children who are able to effectively manage their thinking, attention, and behavior are also more likely to have better grades and higher standardized test scores" (p. 15).

Put simply, when students develop prosocial behaviors and self-regulation skills, they learn more (e.g., Duncan et al., 2007); students with unaddressed problematic behavior learn less (Wilson, Gottfredson, & Najaka, 2001).

Do SEL Programs Co-opt the Role of Parents/Families?

The concern articulated here is that lessons related to SEL teach values. This is true; they do. But we would argue that values are, and have always been, a component of schooling. When a teacher selects a specific book to teach, that choice communicates values. When a teacher responds to a question, the way in which she does so communicates values. When a teacher has students line up boy-girl-boy-girl, this practice communicates values. Schools, and the adults in them and associated with them, intentionally and unintentionally convey their values, morals, and beliefs in every lesson taught. This is an aspect of the *hidden curriculum* (which we will discuss in the next section). It is the reason there is oversight and review. It's why we have school boards and curriculum committees.

When schools and teachers take on SEL in a public and transparent way, the community (including parents and families) can monitor and critique these efforts.

Does SEL Create Groupthink and Uniformity?

Episodically over the years, we have heard SEL described as "communist" or "socialist," and frankly, we remain surprised by this perspective. There is no single way of thinking that is privileged in schools, and SEL programs are no exception. There are appropriate ways of behaving, and there are ways that our society has defined manners and social mores, each with all kinds of nuances and variations.

We believe that efforts to help students grow and develop socially and emotionally, far from being driven by a political agenda, are an indication of teachers working very hard to facilitate the skills their students need to be productive members of society.

SEL as Curriculum

Much of the controversy surrounding SEL seems rooted in concerns about an SEL curriculum's potential to shape students' thinking. In order to explore SEL in the classroom directly, we first need to consider the aspects of *curriculum* as explained by George Posner, one of the world's experts on curriculum theory.

Posner believes that there are at least five levels of any curriculum:

- *The official curriculum*, or written curriculum, gives the basic lesson plan to be followed, including objectives, sequence, and materials. This provides the basis for accountability.
- *The operational curriculum* is what is taught by the teacher, and how it is communicated. This includes what the teacher teaches in class and the learning outcomes for the student.
- *The hidden curriculum* includes the norms and values of the surrounding society. These are stronger and more durable than the first two, and may be in conflict with them.
- *The null curriculum* consists of what is not taught. Consideration must be given to the reasons behind why things are not included in the official or operational curriculum.
- *The extra curriculum* is the planned experiences outside of the specific educational session. (1992, pp. 10–12)

SEL has long existed in the hidden curriculum. This is evidenced any time an adult says, "Boys don't cry" or "Say thank you." Students are learning socially and emotionally all the time, but some of this learning is not productive. If SEL remains part of the hidden curriculum, there will be gaps in students' learning. For example, if students are not directly taught self-regulation strategies, those who have yet to develop these strategies might be marginalized. Teachers might say that a specific student is off task a lot, or distracted, or can't focus. This is an example of the student being blamed for not mastering something he or she was never taught. When all students have been taught self-regulation, teachers can remind them of the strategies to use. As Posner (1992) notes,

> Everything that happens to students influences their lives, and therefore, the curriculum must be considered extremely broadly, not only in terms of what can be planned for students in schools and even outside them, but also in terms of all the unanticipated consequences of each new situation that individuals encounter. The consequences of any situation include not only how it is learned in a formal sense, but also all the thoughts, feelings, and tendencies to action that the situation engenders in those individuals experiencing it. But since each individual differs in at least some small ways from all others, no two individuals can experience the same situation in precisely the same way. (p. 51)

Recognizing SEL as an official component of curriculum allows teachers to operationalize it in their classrooms. Of course, this also opens SEL to the kinds of curricular debates that surround other content areas, including phonics in English language arts, evolution in science, Christopher Columbus in social studies, and procedures versus concepts in math. Any content that is valued as an important part of the schooling experience will be the subject of passionate and differing viewpoints and shaped by the arguments that emerge. In our view, SEL is worthy of the same type of ongoing rigorous debate that has given us the academic curricula that exist today, and like academic curricula, SEL will continue evolving over time.

SEL as Empowerment

Teachers have to teach students how to make decisions about the choices and problems they face. A student who has excellent content knowledge but poor social or problem-solving skills is a student at risk of being manipulated. Similarly, students who are able to predict possible consequences of their actions may be better equipped to make good decisions.

Take, for example, the case of five high-performing high school seniors we knew who were caught smoking marijuana in their hotel rooms while competing in a school-sponsored, statewide competition. These students were very remorseful. In hindsight, they recognized what they had done as a poor decision, but when the choice was in front of them, they "got caught up in the moment" and "didn't think." We know actions do, and should, have consequences. Our point is that these students' *academic* learning was insufficient preparation for a real-world challenge they faced. Among other benefits, helping students build strong social and emotional skills equips them to consider consequences and make good decisions.

Social and emotional learning is not simply about helping students stay out of trouble, though; it's about developing life skills that can be applied to a wide range of situations. Across the examples in this book, you'll find a thread focused on "problems," such as how to work on a team or how to get along with others. One of the major lessons we hope students learn is how to identify problems, analyze problems, and solve problems. To be able to do so, they need to confront a wide range of challenges that are academic, social, and emotional in nature—and their teachers need to equip them with the right tools to engage in these processes. Throughout this book, our intent is to provide teachers with a toolbox of strategies that will help transform students into empowered, all-purpose problem solvers.

In many cases, schools only provide students SEL opportunities through a specific program, and there is evidence that even supplemental programs can help students develop necessary skills (Harrington, Giles, Hoyle, Feeney, & Yungbluth, 2001). In other cases, SEL is the focus of after-school instruction and interventions, which also help students develop their skills (Durlak, Weissberg, & Pachan, 2010). However, what's needed, and what's far less common, is for schools to amplify the principles SEL programs introduce to make them the fabric of the school itself. In order for SEL to have a lasting and sustained effect, it needs to be integrated into the academic mainstream rather than remain on the periphery.

We believe that classroom teachers are critical in this SEL integration effort, and that their intentional moves to develop students' social and emotional skills are crucial. In part, we say this because teachers are already engaged in this type of learning with students through a hidden curriculum. But we also say it because there are so many more students who need to learn these skills to be successful. In an effort to facilitate integration, we have included as an appendix to this book a collection of literary resources for social and emotional learning. The problems real and imaginary characters face provide an opportunity to extend ideas introduced in the SEL program a school is using. Many of the vignettes in the chapters ahead illustrate how teachers can use narrative and informational texts as a springboard for valuable SEL teaching.

In their meta-analysis of 213 SEL programs (involving 270,034 students in grades K–12), Durlak and colleagues (2011) noted that classroom teachers were very effective in implementing SEL. In fact, teacher implementation resulted in statistically significant outcomes on all six factors studied:

- *Social and emotional skills* (effect size = .62). This component focused on "identifying emotions from social cues, goal setting, perspective taking, interpersonal problem solving, conflict resolution, and decision making" (p. 6).
- *Attitudes toward self and others* (effect size = .23). This component included "self-perceptions (e.g., self-esteem, self-concept, and self-efficacy), school bonding (e.g., attitudes toward school and teachers), and conventional (i.e., prosocial) beliefs about violence, helping others, social justice, and drug use" (p. 6).
- *Positive social behavior* (effect size = .26). This category focused on "getting along with others" (p. 6).
- *Conduct problems* (effect size = .20). This category included a range of problematic behaviors including "disruptive class behavior,

noncompliance, aggression, bullying, school suspensions, and delinquent acts" (p. 7).

- *Emotional distress* (effect size = .25). This category focused on internalized mental health issues including "depression, anxiety, stress, or social withdrawal" (p. 7).
- *Academic performance* (effect size = .34). This category included "standardized reading or math achievement test scores" as well as grades in specific classes (p. 7).

Effect sizes are a measure of magnitude, or how much gain is realized based on the influence being studied. The average effect size in educational "influences" relating to learning outcomes is .40 (Hattie, 2009), and as educators, we generally focus on actions, strategies, or practices that are "above average." For example, classroom discussion has an effect size of .82 (Hattie, 2009), so that practice receives acclaim and attention; grade-level retention, on the other hand, is criticized and discouraged due to its negative effect size (–.13).

When teachers teach social and emotional skills, students learn them (effect size of .62). This makes sense, as teaching social and emotional skills should have a direct influence on students' ability to use these skills. But deliberate SEL also has an indirect impact on other facets of a student's life—positively influencing attitudes, social behavior, conduct, levels of distress, and academic performance. Using the .40 criteria, developing students' social and emotional skills is worth the investment of time. However, as Hattie has noted himself, just because a specific influence has an effect size below .40 does not mean it is unworthy of attention. He has focused on academic learning as the outcome and acknowledges that schooling can produce other, very worthy outcomes. We agree.

For example, if teachers can assist students in addressing their mental health issues, it's probably worth the time. One student we knew, Amanda, was socially withdrawn and often anxious. She had few friends and refused to engage in any type of social activity. She saw a psychiatrist twice a week and a school counselor three times a week. Each of these professionals helped Amanda cope with her anxiety and tendency to withdraw from social situations. We are not suggesting that teachers can replace mental health professionals. However, when Amanda's middle school teachers began integrating SEL into their lessons, taking the advice of the professionals and addressing needs naturally in the classroom, Amanda made a lot of progress. She was able to present in front of her English class, complete group projects in science, and attend a school dance (writing in her reflection afterward that she "enjoyed being with other kids and having people to talk to").

Similarly, what teacher out there wouldn't like to see a reduction in problematic behavior, even if it's not at the .40 effect-size level? For most of us, any reduction in the types of behaviors described by Durlak and colleagues (2011) would be welcome. Teaching students how to manage their behavior rather than simply facing consequences for their behavior benefits them in the longer term. We are reminded of Alex, a young man who seemed to always be off task and disruptive. He had a long history of punishment, to the point where his mother told his middle school teachers, "I don't want you calling me anymore. Just suspend him, and I'll deal with it later." She was as frustrated with Alex as his teachers were.

When Alex reached high school, however, he encountered teachers who were accustomed to long-term social skills interventions and did not allow Alex's behavior to rattle them. Instead, each of his teachers spoke to Alex about the effect that his behavior was having on the class. They used circles to provide voice for students in their classes to discuss the learning environment. (In his disruptive early months, Alex's effect on the rest of the class was a topic of discussion in these circles, but so were a wide range of other issues.) Alex's teachers also engaged their students in text selections featuring characters who faced challenges like bullying and peers who were disruptive. They set clear expectations and provided students with opportunities to practice meeting those expectations, including such things as moderating speaking volume, agreed-upon ways to enter the classroom, and what to do when distracted.

By the middle of 9th grade, Alex was no longer the major concern of his grade level. When asked about the change, Alex said, "Yeah, I still get attention, just in other ways. And I kind of like the teachers here, so I don't want their jobs to be harder." By 10th grade, Alex was regularly paying attention in class and taking part in the learning, although there still were days that were hard. When his girlfriend broke up with him, his behavior in class became unacceptable. But rather than ask, "What's wrong with this kid?" his English teacher asked, "What's happened to this kid that's leading him to act this way?" Alex let his teacher know about his heartbreak, and they worked through some plans together.

By the time Alex reached 11th grade, no one could believe he had ever engaged in problematic, disruptive, and disrespectful behavior. He had friends and a part-time job that he loved. He joined the police cadet program, saying, "It's how I can give back." Alex's mom noted that his behavior changed at home as well: "He used to argue all the time and fight with his sister. He's so nice to be around now. I'm really going to miss him when he goes to college."

The moral of this story? Just because a specific influence is below .40 does not mean the approach or strategy is unworthy of attention.

SEL and Equity

It's important to stress that social and emotional learning is about much more than developing kids who are nice to one another, cooperative in class, and civically engaged. SEL is also an equity issue.

Students who lack the communication and regulation skills needed to navigate a complex societal landscape are vulnerable to becoming victims or perpetrators (and sometimes both). These students are often marginalized to the fringes of school and community life, and endure pity, shame, humiliation, and punishment. It is crucial for schools to implement systems that develop students' social and emotional skills so that they can carry, practice, and use these throughout their day, at home when the school day is over, and for the rest of their lives.

We have heard the grumblings that factors educators cannot control are the reason some students behave the way they do. To be sure, poverty and want, neglect and abuse all influence a child's capacity to learn. But our inability to erase such factors cannot become the excuse for doing nothing at all. We can acknowledge the reality of these factors *and* actively work to counteract them. We have also heard the concerns of those who say that some of the skills covered in this book do not reflect the child's home and community environment. They wonder aloud whether they have the right as educators to demand from their students what may not be valued at home.

Here's a case in point. A middle school student at the school where we work opened up a classroom door and shouted a racially abusive epithet. When confronted, he claimed that he was allowed to use that word at home. Now, lots of things happened in response to this incident, including a conference with the student's parents and several restorative meetings with an African American staff member he respects, the teacher who confronted him, and his fellow students. But the very first conversation with the student after the incident was this: you are capable of differentiating your behavior based on the setting. The behaviors one exhibits in a religious house of worship, for instance, are different from those at a sporting event. And an 11-year-old boy is fully capable of telling the difference between home and school, period.

A school that successfully weaves SEL into the fabric of its academic learning and its policies and procedures doesn't get that way by chance. School leaders, staff, and families collaborate with intention to create these conditions. The stakeholders confront troubling issues that bubble just beneath the surface. And they respond proactively to infuse SEL into academic content and social situations. Doing this work, and meeting its many challenges, is only possible if the adults in the school are themselves SEL-competent.

An Integrated SEL Framework

To reiterate, if we want students to learn, if we are willing to do what it takes to help them to learn, and if we believe that appropriate learning targets are more than mastery of core academic content areas, then SEL has to become a deliberate presence in our classrooms.

There have been and continue to be valuable conversations about the merits of particular SEL programs and commercial curricula, but our intention in this book is to address an issue that transcends particulars. We believe that the most important questions to ask about SEL are not about which program to use, but about how teachers will integrate the tenets of SEL into the fabric of their lessons.

Our approach to integrated SEL focuses on delivery at Tier 1, as part of the core instruction and access to grade-level curriculum that every student receives every day. Yes, there will always be students who need more intensive interventions, including those who have experienced trauma or who have challenging disabilities or mental health issues. These students need appropriate interventions and access to experts, generally provided through Tier 2 and Tier 3 supports.

In this book, we offer classroom examples, tools, and strategies that you (or the teachers you work with) can use to intentionally guide students' social and emotional development. We make the case that it is essential to integrate SEL into the academic mainstream of learning. Further, we seek to disrupt the compartmentalized approach to SEL that some schools seem to take, as when standalone lessons occur once a week with little follow-through. Whether using a commercial program or homegrown resources, you need to take advantage of the many opportunities academic learning presents for an integrated SEL approach. We also address the decisions schools must make in order to begin and sustain a meaningful SEL effort.

We have organized the "big ideas" contained under the umbrella of SEL into five broad categories (see Figure 1.1), and which we will discuss in turn and explore more thoroughly in the chapters ahead.

Identity and Agency

Children's and adolescents' sense of identity is shaped by a myriad of factors, including experiences inside and outside school. Their *agency*, which is their belief in their ability to influence the world around them, is materially governed by their identity. Factors that contribute to a young person's identity and agency include

- A recognition of one's strengths.
- The self-confidence to try something new.
- Self-efficacy, or belief in oneself.
- A growth mindset that is fueled by perseverance and grit.
- The resiliency to bounce back from setbacks.

FIGURE 1.1
Integrated SEL

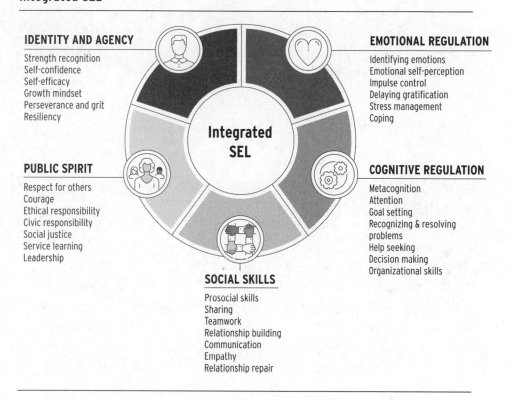

IDENTITY AND AGENCY

Strength recognition
Self-confidence
Self-efficacy
Growth mindset
Perseverance and grit
Resiliency

EMOTIONAL REGULATION

Identifying emotions
Emotional self-perception
Impulse control
Delaying gratification
Stress management
Coping

PUBLIC SPIRIT

Respect for others
Courage
Ethical responsibility
Civic responsibility
Social justice
Service learning
Leadership

COGNITIVE REGULATION

Metacognition
Attention
Goal setting
Recognizing & resolving
problems
Help seeking
Decision making
Organizational skills

SOCIAL SKILLS

Prosocial skills
Sharing
Teamwork
Relationship building
Communication
Empathy
Relationship repair

Emotional Regulation

Students are judged by adults and peers based on how well they regulate their emotions. Those who struggle to regulate their emotions may have difficulty developing and maintaining healthy relationships with others. Skills that positively contribute to emotional regulation include

- Being able to identify and describe emotions.
- Accurately perceiving one's own emotional state as a first step in identifying the emotions of others.
- Learning to manage impulses and delay gratification.
- Recognizing and managing feelings of stress.
- Using adaptive coping skills.

Cognitive Regulation

Learning isn't passive. Acquiring knowledge and skills requires students to engage in certain habits and dispositions. This category of SEL, the one that most closely intersects with the academic instruction we do each day, includes building students' skills in the areas of

- Metacognition
- Sustaining attention
- Goal setting and monitoring
- Recognizing and resolving problems
- Decision making
- Help seeking
- Getting and staying organized

Social Skills

Quality relationships are the basis for effective interactions inside and outside school because they allow for productive and positive collaboration. Students need to be equipped with tools to foster, maintain, and repair relationships, and this requires a substantial amount of adult guidance. In particular, students need to be taught and have opportunities to practice

- Prosocial skills, such as sharing and teamwork
- Building relationships
- Communicating effectively
- Developing and expressing empathy
- Repairing relationships

Public Spirit

This final aspect of our integrated SEL model is the basis for a democratic way of life and essential to creating and sustaining a social structure in which people are valued and treated fairly. We see public spirit evidenced in the ways that people contribute to and steward their communities. Major concepts that help build students' public spirit include

- Having respect for others
- Being courageous
- Understanding one's ethical responsibility
- Recognizing one's civic responsibilities
- Pursuing material improvements in the lives of others through social justice work
- Service learning
- Leadership

Takeaways

All learning is social and emotional, and addressing the skills in our model of SEL has always has been a part of the work educators do, albeit too often unintentionally and as part of the hidden curriculum of the school. The ways in which teachers behave, what we say, the values we express, the materials we chose, and the skills we prioritize all influence how the children and youth in our classroom think, see themselves, interact with others, and assert themselves in the world. Their social and emotional development is too important to be an add-on or an afterthought, too important to be left to chance.

We call on teachers and school leaders to deliberately support the growth of every child, not just academically but also socially and emotionally. Together with their families and community, we can equip them to realize their aspirations and contribute in positive ways to our society. What could be more worthwhile?

CHAPTER 2

Identity and Agency

Strength recognition | Self-confidence
Self-efficacy | Growth mindset
Perseverance and grit | Resiliency

Senaida has a math problem to solve—a big one, filled with all kinds of words, numbers, and symbols. She's been here before. Her teacher, Rolando Cruz, regularly uses rich mathematical tasks to engage his students in complex thinking. He believes that it is important for his students to develop the ability to persevere through a task, as it contributes to their sense of agency. He also wants each of his students to develop a self-efficacious identity as a learner; if this is reinforced in other classes, they will develop a life skill that will serve them well.

Senaida takes a moment, looking at the challenging problem in front of her. She turns the paper over so it's facedown on her desk, closes her eyes, and takes a deep breath. When she opens her eyes, she flips the paper back over and rereads the problem. Like all the students in Mr. Cruz's class, she's learned to think aloud so that her peers and teacher can offer assistance, as needed. Softly, Senaida says, "I'm feeling stressed when I read this. I feel myself getting a little anxious, thinking that I'm not going to be able to figure it out." She pauses for a few moments and takes another deep breath. "And then I think I'm going to fail. And then I think about being embarrassed . . . and about my mom being disappointed in me."

Hearing her, Anthony leans over and says, "Hide it under your book for a minute and just try to visualize what the task is asking you. Think about what the problem is all about."

Senaida does just that. She hides the paper under her math book and closes her eyes again. She raises her index fingers to her temples, a sign that Mr. Cruz has taught his students to indicate to him that they are thinking deeply and that he doesn't need to offer help just yet.

When she opens her eyes, Senaida says, "I think I need to figure out the perimeter first. If I know that, then I can figure out how much sidewalk there would be and then how much space there would have to be for the swimming pool." Retrieving her paper from underneath her book, Senaida reads the task again. This time, she underlines and circles specific lines in the text and makes some marginal notes that include her thoughts. She then draws a model and starts labeling the parts. After several minutes of work, Senaida looks up and says to Anthony, "Thanks. I just needed that reminder about what I know and can do."

A person's personal identity and sense of agency is the foundation of his or her emotional life. As human beings, how we see ourselves and our belief in our capacity to act upon our immediate world affect every waking moment of our lives.

Agency and identity can be relatively stable or unstable, and they are influenced positively and negatively by circumstances, environment, and (as Senaida realized) the people around us and the challenges we face. Students' identity and agency are shaped by educators' words and actions (whether intentional or not). As educators, paying mindful attention to the development of our students' identity and agency is beneficial because it is foundational to their learning and achievement. A child who is not confident is unlikely to take intellectual risks. Students with a diminished sense of agency can't fathom that there is anything they can do to change the trajectory of their learning. Investment in each student's identity and agency pays off in academics and in their accomplishments.

Identity and Agency Defined

Each of us holds a self-concept and a related set of beliefs about our ability to act upon the world. *Identity* is an understanding of who we are—our attributes, the way we see ourselves in relation to others, our perceived talents, and the awareness of our shortcomings. It is the narrative we tell the world and ourselves about ourselves. *Agency* describes our capacity to act in empowered and autonomous ways. Beliefs about our agency influence confidence and contribute to our resiliency when faced with a negative event. Both identity and agency are influenced by fixed and fluid structures such as gender, race, sexual orientation, experiences, culture, and socioeconomic status.

As noted, identity is not static; it is continually shaped and redefined over a lifetime. Experiences can have a profound effect on one's identity, as can the stories we tell ourselves about the experiences we have. Consider how a shift in language might change how people who have experienced trauma process the occurrence: are they *victims* of abuse, or *survivors* of abuse? Identity is further understood through interactions with others. We construct our notions of self by using the mirror others hold up to us. We watch how others react to us and listen for the language they use to describe us. Family and peers influence identity formation, as do experiences in school.

Teachers' words and actions have a great deal to do with how students form their identities. Johnston (2004) notes, "Teachers' comments can offer them, and nudge them toward, productive identities" (p. 23). We can also negatively impact a child's identity, even unintentionally. A 1st grade teacher we observed was demonstrating an online reading practice system for her students—one that assesses reading proficiency and then assigns reading tasks based on current level of performance (using the alphabet to level readers). Such programs provide an opportunity for distributed practice in reading. However, in showing her students how to complete tasks, the teacher logged into the account of the student who read at the lowest level in the class. The little girl's reading level, projected on the screen alongside her name, revealed her to be at Level B. The other students in the class started whispering to each other: "Is she really on B?" and "That's really low. I'm at M, so B is really bad." The child whose reading score was displayed refused for weeks after to log into the system to practice reading. Unfortunately, the teacher's action had triggered a new identity—"I'm a bad reader, and everyone knows it"—and damaged the child's relationships with fellow students.

Agency is necessarily tied to identity, as it describes a person's capacity to take action and shape his or her destiny. Like identity, a sense of agency is socially constructed. A young person's social networks of family, friends, school, and community—called *social capital*—influences his or her sense of agency. Students with strong social capital gain a sense of autonomy because their network of relationships keeps them feeling emotionally and psychologically safe; this helps them feel comfortable enough to take calculated risks and try new things in the classroom, like working through problems and testing solutions. But students with weak social capital feel less secure. They might engage in risky behavior (like guessing) or fail to act when they should because they feel alone and exposed. Students with a limited sense of agency show it. They may be immobilized, feel angry, blame others, or even lash out. The good news is that teachers can guide students toward a greater sense of agency by lighting a path for taking action and getting results.

Consider Drew, a 9th grade student who was not yet as academically skilled as his classmates and had grown accustomed to comparing himself negatively to others. Because he didn't consider himself smart or capable, he had a history of giving up easily when he faced a challenge in the classroom. It was the kind of behavior some teachers would see as a sign that Drew was "lazy and unmotivated," which is exactly what his 8th grade English teacher wrote on his report card. But things changed for Drew when he enrolled in a new school—one that is integrating social and emotional learning in the classroom and one where teachers like Luz Avila take this charge seriously.

Ms. Avila teaches English. When Drew read the writing prompt she distributed, which focused on the first few chapters of George Orwell's *Animal Farm*, he put his head down on the table. Ms. Avila noticed, and when she checked in with Drew, he was honest. "It's just too hard," he said quietly. "I'm reading the book, and it's OK, but I don't know what 'the contradictions' are, or even what that word means. I don't know what Orwell is trying to say, and I don't want to do this. I'll just fail. That's what I do."

Ms. Avila, knowing that challenging tasks can be a trigger for students with identity and agency struggles, responded by starting a friendly conversation with Drew and asking him a few questions about the text:

- What are some of the ways in which the animals changed between Chapters 1 and 6?
- How did Napoleon become more powerful?
- Why did Napoleon tell the other animals that Snowball was responsible for the ruin of the windmill?
- Why does Napoleon have the dogs guard him?

Drew had answers to all of these questions, and he even seemed to be enjoying the conversation. Ms. Avila pointed out, "What I'm hearing is that you know a lot about this book. And those are some really interesting ideas about how dictators develop. As you say, it happened slowly, and more animals had to go to Napoleon for answers." She suggested to Drew that he use this knowledge and apply it to the writing prompt. "Would it help if we took the prompt apart and figured out the task together?" she asked. In that moment, Ms. Avila pivoted from supporting Drew academically to supporting him academically *and* emotionally.

Drew confessed that what he really wanted to know was the meaning of the word *contradiction*. "I think I got stuck when I read that word, and not knowing it made me feel like I was going to fail."

Yes, it's true. A detail as small as the meaning of a single word in a prompt can stop a student with a limited sense of agency in his tracks. But talking with students like Drew, and listening closely to spot when their agency is threatened, can help you to show them ways they can get themselves restarted.

Recognizing Strengths

There is little evidence that learning preference or learning style inventories work (Peterson & Meissel, 2015). There is no evidence that asking students if they are kinesthetic or auditory learners will help you teach them any better, or that they are likely to acquire any more knowledge when instruction is aligned to those styles. What, then, do we mean when we advise you to help your students learn to recognize their strengths?

Here's a simple test we like to give students. The first thing we do is ask them to think of a particular subject, and when they've done that, we ask, "In what parts of this subject do you really stink?" (Sometimes we phrase this more politely, asking them where they "perform poorly.") We have never met a student who could not provide a long list of areas of struggle and failure. Then we ask, "In that same subject, what are your strengths?" We get far fewer responses comparatively. Frequently, students reply with nothing but a blank stare.

Fourth grader Aaron is just one of many examples. Aaron was able to provide a long list of the areas of mathematics where he performed poorly, starting with "I'm not good at math. I'm not good at my times tables. And fractions are not so good. I do them wrong a lot. My dad gets pretty frustrated." When we asked Aaron his strengths in mathematics, he shrugged. "Like I said, I'm not good at math. But I'm good at Minecraft."

That students can so readily point out their failings shouldn't be so surprising. As teachers (and parents, to be honest), we tend to focus on weaknesses, gaps in learning, and deficits. We're looking to see where we need to step in, where we might help. And because we want students to understand that failure is an opportunity to learn, we tend to highlight errors that can guide them toward new learning. But to support positive identity development and agency, we should also be highlighting students' strengths and all the evidence of mastery they're showing us.

One way to do that is through feedback. When Hattie and Timperley (2007) analyzed feedback, they noted that there were four types teachers (and parents and peers) might employ:

- *Corrective feedback*, which is feedback about the task itself (i.e., the accuracy of the response). For obvious reasons, this isn't very effective for helping students identify strengths.
- *Feedback about the processing of the task*, which focuses on the ways in which the student approached the task. This type of feedback is a great choice for helping students recognize strengths such as effort, strategy

choice, focus, perseverance, and progress. It is also a very effective way to approach identity-related struggles, often voiced as "I'm just not good at this."

- *Feedback about self-regulation*, which focuses on students' ability to manage their emotions and behavior during a specific situation. This type of feedback is another good choice for helping students recognize strengths. Used to acknowledge their actions, choices, and responses, it can boost their sense of agency.

- *Feedback about the person*, which focuses on praise about the individual's character traits. This type of feedback is rarely effective, especially when it's vague praise like "You always do a great job" or "You are smart." Although we don't want to discourage praise, it shouldn't be confused with feedback. Unlike feedback, praise doesn't give a student any direction as to what to do next, or any information about why something he or she did was successful.

Note that all four types of feedback can, and should, be used for academics; what we want to highlight here is how deploying them in the right circumstances is a way to integrate social and emotional skill development into your existing instruction. Figure 2.1 provides examples of each of these types of feedback and summarizes their effectiveness in contexts where you want to address social and emotional learning as well as content mastery.

There are ways beyond feedback to help students identify their strengths. For example, in her 1st grade classroom, Jennifer Herrera has her students rotate through a number of different classroom jobs, such as materials manager, table captain, technology support, lunch counter, and so on. She meets with students after their three-week rotation to pinpoint aspects of their job performance that were particularly successful. As Ms. Herrera told us, "I want them to know that there are things that they are really good at and things that they have to work at to improve. I keep them in jobs for several weeks to make sure that they really understand the role. But I also want to help them be able to advocate for themselves in the future."

FIGURE 2.1

Types of Feedback and Their Effectiveness

Type of Feedback	Examples	Effectiveness
About the task (*Corrective feedback*)	"You need to be seated in your chair with your book ready." "Yes, you need to share that with your partner."	Effective when addressing mistakes in content learning, but not when the learner lacks knowledge or skill. Not effective for behavior corrections.
About the processing of the task	"I noticed that you focused on this task for 12 minutes without giving up or becoming distracted." "Did you notice how much more you learned when you were practicing your active listening strategies?"	Very effective, as it labels the cognitive and metacognitive strategies the learner is using or should be using.
About self-regulation	"I saw you were frustrated with your group, but you gave them feedback and it seemed to work to get everyone back on track." "You were really excited about your ideas in your science lab. I saw that you held back a bit to let your team members share their ideas, too. You didn't dominate, even though you understood it faster than the others. That gave them time to figure it out, too."	Very effective, as it helps learners to self-assess their ability, actions, and knowledge.
About the person	"Well done." "You are such a good kid."	Ineffective, because it doesn't yield task-specific information.

Michael Perez also works to help his students identify their strengths. For each major assignment in his 6th grade class, he creates a checklist of strengths (from his master list of 20 items) that students can practice or demonstrate as part of their learning. For example, their lesson on ancient China's contributions to the world included the following self-assessment statements:

- I can help peers without telling them the answer.
- I can summarize readings effectively.
- I can keep track of time so that my group finishes tasks.

- I can illustrate ideas and concepts in powerful ways.
- I can follow directions and explain directions to others.
- I can make sure that everyone has a chance to speak in our group.

Notice how these statements are crafted to contribute to students' sense of identity and specifically foster agency. Mr. Perez also asks his students to identify one area of strength that they would like to develop, and he works individually with them to develop a plan for this growth. His use of these success criteria not only provides students with academic targets but empowers students to pursue and attain them.

Ninth grade English teacher Joon Yi's unit assessments include a blank page at the end with the heading: *Here are other things I know about this unit of study that you didn't ask on the test.* His students are free to add anything they choose that is related to the unit and potentially earn points that count toward their grade for the exam. "I am constantly surprised by the depth of understanding and the sophisticated connections they make to other concepts," he told us. Mr. Yi's students benefit by earning extra points by demonstrating mastery of the content, and Mr. Yi uses the material they provide to improve his assessments year over year. He credits their insights with making him a better teacher.

Self-Confidence

The poet e. e. cummings is widely quoted as saying that "once we believe in ourselves, we can risk curiosity, wonder, spontaneous delight, or any experience that reveals the human spirit." Students need to believe in themselves if they are to truly engage in learning; teachers, in turn, need to help students develop self-confidence.

As we write this, we are reminded that there are some students—like a certain high school senior we'll call Ahmed—who seems to have no shortage of self-confidence. Some people say Ahmed is cocky and arrogant, and others dismiss him because he is always telling them about his accomplishments. The truth is, Ahmed is overconfident in his abilities, and it has a troubling effect on his learning. He is dismissive of the knowledge of others, including his teachers. He spends less time studying than his classmates, and he seems less motivated to learn. The consequences of Ahmed's overconfidence are consistent with the findings of Dunlosky and Rawson (2012), who report that overconfident students achieve at lower levels due to a resistance to being open to the ideas of others.

Underconfident learners, on the other hand, doubt that they possess the internal resources such as ability and perseverance, and question the usefulness of external resources, such as teacher guidance, when it comes to completing tasks (Stirin, Ganzach, Pazy, & Eden, 2012).

Self-confidence is evidenced in outward behaviors (see Figure 2.2). Truly self-confident people do not feel the need to tell others about their accomplishments. They also freely admit mistakes, because they know that mistakes are learning experiences. People who are self-confident accept compliments, are not dismissive about the recognition that they receive, and accurately recognize the internal and external resources that help them achieve their goals.

FIGURE 2.2.
Confidence Behaviors

Confident Behavior	Behavior Associated with Lower Self-Confidence
Doing what you believe to be right, even if others tease or criticize you for it	Acting in certain ways because you worry about what other people think
Being willing to take reasonable risks and put forth effort to achieve better things	Staying in your comfort zone, fearing failure, and avoiding risks
Admitting your mistakes and learning from them	Working hard to cover up mistakes and hoping that you can fix the problem before anyone notices
Waiting for others to congratulate you on your accomplishments	Talking about your successes as often as possible and with as many people as possible
Accepting compliments graciously ("Thanks, I really worked hard on that essay. I'm pleased you recognize my efforts.")	Dismissing compliments offhandedly ("Oh that essay was nothing, really; anyone could have done it.")

Source: Adapted with permission from *Building Self-Confidence: Preparing Yourself for Success!* by MindTools; retrieved from https://www.mindtools.com/selfconf.html

Self-confidence is associated with resiliency, itself a protective factor for dealing with emotional abuses, stress, and trauma (Ungar, 2008). Children and adolescents who are first-generation citizens of a nation also draw on self-confidence to navigate the cross-cultural terrain of home and school (Ungar et al., 2007).

One question that's valuable to consider is where self-confidence comes from. Some of it is person-specific, but self-confidence is also *domain-specific*, meaning that it varies by task. False praise—that is, praise that exceeds the level of accomplishment—does not build the kind of self-confidence that allows learning to thrive. Effective teacher feedback, on the other hand (see Figure 2.1) and appropriately structured learning tasks, such as micro-skill lessons (Macgowan & Wong, 2017), can help students accurately calibrate their self-confidence relative to their internal and external resources. There is evidence that supportive peers also lead to better self-confidence (Lee, Ybarra, Gonzalez, & Ellsworth, 2018).

Maclellan (2014), who reviewed the research literature on teachers' actions to develop self-confidence in learners, recommends that teachers do the following:

- Encourage student engagement through socially designed learning activities that promote self-concept as well as facilitate the development of knowledge.
- Plan activities in which students have to explain their reasoning and debate the evidence on which they make their claims.
- Embed self-regulative and metacognitive activities [see Chapter 4] in all lessons.
- Engage in dialogic feedback with students. (p. 68)

Teacher Elan Ramos has a quote from Eleanor Roosevelt framed on his classroom wall: "No one can make you feel inferior without your consent." Mr. Ramos often refers to the quote before students engage in complex tasks or before they provide feedback to one another. He also routinely focuses on confidence as part of his lessons. For example, we observed a classroom discussion in which he invited students to talk about ways they might stay focused and calm while making a presentation. "Public speaking requires skills that we don't use every day," he told them. "Let's create a list of things we can do to keep calm and maintain our confidence." This was direct and deliberate work to address the issue of self-confidence as a contributor to students' success. Mr. Ramos's group went on to identify strategies they could use when they felt their confidence was compromised.

As part of any effort to integrate SEL into everyday instruction, it's necessary to monitor students' confidence levels, be mindful of the language you use (so that you don't unintentionally undermine anyone's confidence), and (like Mr. Ramos does) provide students with strategies that they can use to build and maintain their confidence.

Self-Efficacy

Self-efficacy is a measure of the belief in one's ability to take action (agency), complete a task, and attain goals (Bandura, 2001). It influences self-confidence and is, in turn, influenced by one's skill sets. A challenge in understanding self-efficacy's effect on learning is that it is something of a two-way street, what Talsma, Schüz, Schwarzer, and Norris (2018) call "the chicken-and-egg conundrum": "I believe, therefore I achieve. I achieve, therefore I believe" (p. 137). The second construct, the idea that performance informs belief, can be promoted in the classroom through the use of *mastery learning* (learning for the sake of learning) and individual goal setting (see Chapter 4). A mastery orientation reduces the need for social comparison to others to boost self-confidence.

How can teachers influence students' self-belief to enhance learning and goal attainment? Consider that an important factor in self-efficacy is believing that the task is within your capacity, and a step toward that belief is seeing someone else complete the task successfully—particularly someone like you. For this reason, compiling short video clips of students performing various tasks—and highlighting the keys to success—can be a very effective support for both short-term task completion and long-term development of self-efficacy. For example, a 3rd grade teacher might help this year's class to build confidence in their ability to master multiplication by sharing written or recorded reflections from last year's class on the progress they made and what they can now do. A physics teacher might decorate the walls of the physic lab with photographs of student teams working step by step through the creative and iterative process of building a solar-powered miniature vehicle.

You can also use literature to build self-efficacy by choosing books that carry a message about belief in oneself. Books like *Amazing Grace* (Hoffman, 1991; for elementary students) and *Giraffes Can't Dance* (Andreae, 2012; for preschool children) profile characters who refuse to accept other people's notions of what they can and cannot do. Older students can see self-efficacy unfold in books like *The Skin I'm In* (Flake, 2007), which features a female protagonist who combats bullying and racism and finds her own voice.

Once again, a teacher's mindful use of language can also help to build a student's self-efficacy. "It's the power of *yet*," explained high school mathematics teacher Frida Gomez, noting that a lot of the concepts in her class are intellectually challenging. "I've got kids who come in with a low sense of self-efficacy when it comes to math. When I hear any of them saying they can't do something, I always tell them, 'You meant to say you can't do it *yet*. That's why you have me.'"

Growth Mindset

At its most basic level, *mindset* is the attitude that someone holds about a task. For example, we all have a mindset about exercise. For some of us, exercise is a necessary evil; for others, it's an integral part of our lives. And for still others, it's something to avoid at all cost. Our actions are rooted in our mindset. For someone who believes that exercise is a necessary evil, there isn't a lot of pleasure in working out, but the task still gets done. For someone who sees exercise as integral, workouts are scheduled and enjoyable. Someone with an "exercise is essential" mindset is also more likely to talk about their exercise goals and successes.

In the classroom, mindset is an expression of identity, agency, and self-efficacy as it applies to learning. Carol Dweck's 2006 best-selling book *Mindset* introduced many educators to idea of *fixed* and *growth* mindsets. According to Dweck, people with a fixed mindset believe their basic qualities, including intelligence and talent, are unchanging and unchangeable traits. Believing that talent alone creates success, they discount the effort involved in mastering something new. To them, they either "get it" or they don't—and when they don't get it (whatever *it* is), they give up. People with a fixed mind-set approach situations with doubt and questions, such as, "Will I succeed or fail? Will I look smart or dumb? Will I be accepted or rejected? Will I feel like a winner or a loser?" (Dweck, 2006, p. 6). These self-doubting questions are tangled up in self-confidence and grounded in social comparison.

People with a growth mindset, on the other hand (see Figure 2.3), believe that their basic abilities can be developed through focused efforts, dedication, and hard work. They persevere, seeing failure as temporary and something to be overcome, not as a reflection of their intelligence or talents. As Dweck notes, "The passion for stretching yourself and sticking to it, even (or especially) when it's not going well, is the hallmark of the growth mindset. This is the mindset that allows people to thrive during some of the most challenging times in their lives" (2006, p. 7).

But it is not as simple as saying that Angel, Ariana, and Carlos have fixed mindsets, whereas Andrew, Hector, and Chastity have growth mindsets. The reality is that all of us—and all of our students—have elements of both fixed and growth mindsets. A mindset changes based on the content area, topic, experience, past success, and environmental factors. For example, you can have a generally growth-oriented mindset toward reading, yet a book that is difficult for you to understand may trigger a fixed mindset. It is not all one or all the other.

There is emerging evidence that general mindset interventions are not especially effective for many students. Sisk, Burgoyne, Sun, Butler, and Macnamara (2018) conducted two meta-analyses, the first of which involved 273 studies on mindset involving more than 365,000 children, adolescents, and adults. They found a weak relationship between a learner's mindset and academic achievement. The second meta-analysis on mind-set interventions was smaller (43 studies involving 57,000 participants). Again, they reported a small effect size ($d = .08$) indicating little influence (see Chapter 1's discussion of effect sizes). However, the most important finding was that there was a somewhat stronger positive effect on

FIGURE 2.3
Fixed Versus Growth Mindset

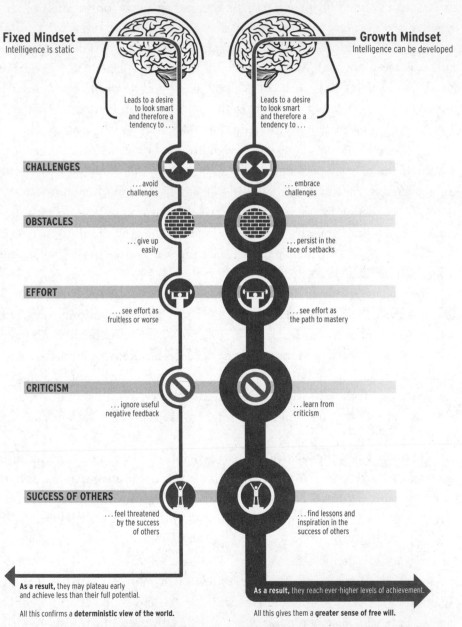

Source: Reprinted with permission from *Carol Dweck: A Summary of The Two Mindsets and the Power of Believing That You Can Improve.* Original graphic by Nigel Holmes. Copyright 2015 by Carol Dweck.

students who had been previously identified as being at high academic risk and who lived in poverty. The second was that interactive interventions that involved application through writing and discussion were more effective than passive ones that only required students to read about mindset. Sisk and colleagues recommended that mindset interventions targeting high-risk students, in combination with other SEL interventions, might amplify the effect. However, in isolation, and when applied to all learners (including those who already possessed a growth mindset about a topic or task), the effect was near zero—and in a few studies, actually had a detrimental effect (Sisk et al., 2018).

In light of these results, we recommend that teachers reexamine the use of mindset interventions to more precisely target those students who are at significant risk for failure and who live in poverty. In addition, mindset interventions should be framed within the larger context of global SEL efforts. Teachers can support students' development of a growth mindset by helping them recognize the triggers that cause them to shift from a growth to a fixed mindset, and then identifying strategies they can use to refocus on learning.

Perseverance and Grit

Perseverance is thought of primarily as an internal construct that describes the willingness to stick with a challenge. *Grit* is an outward expression of this—how one shows persistence toward a goal, the ability to "give up a lot of other things in order to do it, [demonstrating] deep commitments that you remain loyal to over many years" (Perkins-Gough & Duckworth, 2013, p. 16). Children and adolescents draw on perseverance and grit when they invest in long-term goals like playing a musical instrument, engaging in a sport, or excelling at an academic subject. The curriculum is replete with opportunities to develop perseverance. Consider, for example, how rich mathematical tasks that require students to hang with a problem for an extended period of time encourage perseverance, or what Bray (2014) calls "being a doer of hard things" (p. 5).

Don't underestimate the influence of encountering characters that exhibit similar qualities. In one study of persistence and role-play (White et al., 2017), researchers asked 4- to 6-year-olds to engage in a repetitive computer task that the researchers acknowledged was boring. They also offered the subjects the option of playing another video game—one that was highly engaging—if they wanted to take a break. The children who were asked to imagine themselves as persistent characters like Dora the Explorer or Batman stuck with the boring task at a rate 46 percent higher than those who were not asked to role-play.

What implication does this have? One is that students should regularly encounter fictional and real characters in their reading who exhibit qualities we want students to try on and perhaps adopt. Many of the titles that 3rd grade teacher Neli Beltran uses for her daily "short book talk" feature characters who demonstrate grit. These book talks have the added benefit of "blessing the book," marking various titles with the teacher's stamp of approval and making them more appealing to students (Marinak & Gambrell, 2016). Ms. Beltran provides a brief overview, tailoring her remarks to her students' interests. She then makes the book available to anyone who would like to read it during independent reading time, which follows the book talk. Current favorites of hers include *Salt in His Shoes* (Jordan & Jordan, 2003), written by basketball great Michael Jordan's mother and sister, and *Ada Twist, Scientist* (Beaty, 2016), about a girl's use of science experiments to answer questions about the world. "I like to reinforce a message about the power of diligence and a strong work ethic as a path for learning," Ms. Beltran told us.

She added that individual persistence and grit aren't enough; they should be leveraged to better the lives of others. In her book talk about *A Chair for My Mother* (Williams, 1982), she tells her students that she first learned about this book when she was a little girl, watching *Reading Rainbow*. The story of a family's loss of their possessions due to a house fire, and the daughter's determination to save her money to buy her hardworking mother a new chair, is important for students to know. "What seems to matter to the kids are the contributions everyone makes. I want them to know that they can help others through their perseverance and grit."

Another aspect of perseverance and grit is locating one's passion and using it to drive effort. Youth scouting organizations are dedicated to helping children and adolescents find their interests using a merit badge system. Those of us who have been in such organizations know the motivation that comes from filling a sash with badges that signify our accomplishments. But the secret to such systems is that they encourage students to try things they might not otherwise have accomplished. Middle school English teacher Adrienne Huston introduced the video game Road Not Taken to her students after reading the Robert Frost poem of the same name. It is a rogue-like puzzle game, meaning that it involves role-play and progression through a series of increasingly difficult challenges. The goals are to explore different paths in life and to rescue children. "The level systems in these kinds of games are great for encouraging kids to take on harder tasks. But what really seems to move them forward is earning badges," she said. "In this game, there are badges called Lived a Good Life, Good Samaritan, Healer, and Lore Master. There are so many students playing it that we now have an informal after-school gaming club!"

Resiliency

Resiliency is the ability to overcome challenges. Students naturally encounter a variety of challenges, from exams that they think they will fail to trauma they have witnessed or experienced. Some challenges are personal, and others are more public. Resilient people are able to bounce back from setbacks and are often stronger or wiser as a result. Of course, we all want to reduce and prevent trauma that our students experience so they don't have to "bounce back." But the fact remains that students will encounter a wide range of challenges in their lives.

To stay on top of what his students are facing, Dominique logs his morning interactions with them. In a single day, before school had even started, he encountered students who were

- Victims of child abuse, living in foster care, worried about getting kicked out.
- Facing food insecurity and hoarding breakfast in the cafeteria.
- Stressing over an interaction with a boss at work the night before.
- Crying in the stairwell after a breakup with a girlfriend.
- Dealing with the death of a parent.

- Worrying about a failed test and needing a plan for academic recovery.
- Stewing over racist comments directed at them by a passenger on a public bus.

And these are just the students who decided to say something that morning. Imagine all of the challenges students face in a given day. Imagine the ones they don't tell us about. It's impressive that they learn anything at all, given what else is on their minds. As teachers, we can help more of these students learn, and learn better, if we understand the value of social and emotional learning and focus specifically on building resiliency.

Some of the protective factors for the range of challenges human beings experience are personal characteristics. It's true that some people have a hopeful outlook by nature and look for the positive in every situation. But some do not. Even those of us who are naturally positive can be thwarted by major challenges. We had a student—a very well-adjusted young man who excelled in school—who had previously exhibited quite a bit of resiliency. He had experienced a number of setbacks in life, but the death of his mother was too much. This otherwise positive and productive young person was in an understandably dark place. He cried nearly every day and was worried about what his peers would think of him for doing so. He neglected his schoolwork and spent his time in class doodling on paper. All students need help at some point in time; as teachers, we never know when a student will need the resiliency skills we teach.

Resiliency quizzes such as the one in Figure 2.4 are useful in raising the topic of resiliency, identifying its components, and developing plans to build or rebuild it. (This particular tool is intended for adolescents. For younger students, we recommend the PBS online tool featuring the animated character Arthur, at https://pbskids.org/arthur/health/resilience/quiz.html.) However, such quizzes do not, in and of themselves, increase students' resiliency.

The actual work is done by integrating resiliency lessons into our classrooms. Henderson (2013) has a name for schools that prioritize this work: *safe-haven schools*. Teachers in safe-haven schools enact practices that result in more resilient people, because they build students' internal and environmental protective factors.

FIGURE 2.4
Resiliency Quiz

Physiological and Emotional Regulation					
Rate each item on a scale of 1-5. Select the answer that best describes how you respond to stress.	Less true			More true	
1. I feel overwhelmed one or more times a day.	1	2	3	4	5
2. When something is bugging me, I usually know what it is and why.	1	2	3	4	5
3. I encourage myself in stressful situations just as I'd encourage a friend.	1	2	3	4	5
4. I am able to step back and laugh even when difficult things happen.	1	2	3	4	5
5. Generally, I have healthy coping mechanisms for handling stress.	1	2	3	4	5

Thinking Style

Pick the statement in each pair that most represents your attitude.

6. When it comes to test taking . . .
    ☐ If you study hard and prepare well, there is almost never such a thing as an unfair test.
    ☐ Teachers often give such random questions that studying too much seems pointless.

7. When it comes to "making it" in life . . .
    ☐ Success has more to do with hard work than luck.
    ☐ It is more who you know than what you know that counts in life.

8. When it comes to getting along with others . . .
    ☐ Developing good relationships with others is a skill that can be learned.
    ☐ Some people just can't form good relationships.

9. When it comes to understanding my part in problems . . .
    ☐ I have a good sense of accurate personal responsibility in most situations.
    ☐ I often assume the worst in situations and wonder why things have gotten so bad.

Meaning in Life

Choose the response to the following sentences that most closely matches how you currently think.

10. When it comes to priorities . . .
     ☐ Staying happy is my top priority.
     ☐ Sticking to my values is my top priority.
11. When it comes to self-knowledge . . .
     ☐ I know myself, my strengths, and my preferences pretty well.
     ☐ My sense of myself, my strengths, and my preferences seems to vary a lot.

continued

FIGURE 2.4 (continued)
Resiliency Quiz

12. I am looking for something that makes my life meaningful.
   ☐ In time. Right now I'm just seeking fun.
   ☐ Yes, I'm not sure what it is or how to find it.
   ☐ No. Life does not really hold any big meaning, so why waste time looking?
   ☐ Yes, and I am pursuing something right now that is very meaningful.

Questions 1–5 assess your current physiological and emotional responses to stressful situations. If you are frequently overwhelmed or unhappy with how you handle stress, then it is time to improve this area of your personal resilience profile. Relaxation, meditation, and mindfulness skills can greatly improve your ability to handle stress. Research also reveals that you can build greater resilience by artfully identifying and conveying emotions while treating yourself and others with compassion.

Questions 6–9 examine your attitude about your actions. Some options suggest more resilience than others. Resilient individuals think their actions matter and that they can function effectively. They also know the importance of developing good interpersonal skills for managing relationships.

Questions 10–12 assess your sense of purpose in life, which might include spiritual beliefs as well as humanitarian values.

Note: This quiz is intended solely to pique the reader's interest in assessing level of personal resiliency and does not have validated psychometric properties.

Source: Adapted with permission from *The Resiliency Quiz* by James F. Huntington. Copyright 2016 by James F. Huntington.

These protective factors include

- Caring relationships with teachers and mentors.
- Clear and consistent structures, such as classroom routines and a tone of civility.
- Exposure to stories of others overcoming diversity.
- Mirroring students' strengths back to them.
- Opportunities to help and serve others.

Some of these practices are easy to implement, whereas others are more complex. The point is to develop students' sense of agency and self-efficacy so that they have skills that they can use when they are faced with a challenge. This can be as simple as selecting texts that feature resilient characters. The message in the classic story *The Little Engine That Could* is powerful for students, but it needs to be discussed. The point of the story is not about the train, but the effort that the train put forth to achieve the goal. Older students might read Tupac Shakur's poem, "The Rose That Grew from Concrete" (1999), as a basis for discussions about perseverance and resiliency. When teacher Joel Perez shared the Tupac poem with his students, he asked them to identify the "concrete" in their lives and how they will break through that concrete to grow. To be sure, one lesson on one text will not develop resiliency, but regular doses of texts that provide examples of strategies that can be used might change a life.

In addition, teachers can ask students, "What's the hard part?" in relation to any content-related task, assignment, or activity. With practice, students can start to identify the hard part of any situation they are in. Sarah Green asks her 4th grade students to identify the hard part of every task they do, deliberately developing this as a habit and a skill to apply when confronted with challenges. This was the case when Kanella's dog died and she was crying in class. Kanella said, "The hardest part is missing her. She was supersick, but I really miss her." Ms. Green shared her own experience with loss and invited Kanella to create a digital picture book so that she could keep the memories. Learning to identify the "hard parts," and then address them, builds resiliency and allows students to process their experiences.

 ## WHEN STUDENTS NEED MORE SUPPORT . . .

We believe that teachers can integrate resilience-building activities into their classrooms and provide students with tools to address the challenges that arise in their lives. However, when trauma and serious adverse childhood events are present, we also know that students need professional help from a qualified person.

Teachers are the eyes and ears of child protection, mental health, and family support services. It's important to be on the lookout for signs of trauma so that students can get help and persist even though something has happened to them. Some of the symptoms of trauma in children closely mimic depression, including too much or too little sleep; loss of appetite or overeating; unexplained irritability and anger; and problems focusing on projects, schoolwork, and conversation.

There is a problematic statement that is often repeated in these situations: "That which doesn't kill you makes you stronger." We don't subscribe to that theory. Rather, we understand that we, as teachers, share the responsibility with family members and mental health professionals in helping students compensate for the negative and traumatic experiences they have.

Takeaways

An underlying principle of social and emotional learning is developing the identity and agency of students in ways that open them up to learning. Teachers can assist children and adolescents in developing the ability to recognize their strengths and accurately weigh current abilities with knowledge of their internal and external resources. When this is done well, students develop a level of self-confidence and self-efficacy that fuels learning while reducing factors that get in the way. Perseverance and grit factor into young people's developing confidence and sense of efficacy, in turn empowering students and building their resiliency in the face of challenge. At the heart of these practices are caring educators and school leaders who commit to the social and emotional learning of the young people in their charge.

 QUESTIONS FOR REFLECTION

1. What opportunities do you see in your content to integrate identity and agency into your practice?
2. What techniques do you use to help your students recognize their strengths?
3. What conversations do you have with your students regarding self-confidence? What techniques and language do you use to help student recalibrate their estimate of self-confidence when it is too low or too high?
4. How do you integrate elements of self-efficacy into your content instruction? In what ways might your content be useful for building student beliefs about their efficacy?

5. What is the current level of understanding in your grade level, department, or school about the nuances of mindset, beyond knowledge of fixed and growth mindsets? In what ways do your students learn about triggers that can shift them into a fixed mindset?

6. Do you discuss resiliency with your students? What professional resources do you have in your school and district to assist students who need further professional intervention due to trauma?

CHAPTER 3

Emotional Regulation

Identifying emotions | Emotional self-perception | Impulse control | Delaying gratification | Stress management | Coping

"Yes, Tyler?" Ms. Ramirez says, pausing her reading to acknowledge one of her 1st graders, who is waving his hand in the air.

"Oliver is playing with his Pokémon cards."

Ms. Ramirez glances over at Oliver, who has quickly put his hands under his desk. "Oliver, we've talked about this," she says. "You should be paying attention to the book I'm reading. Please go move your clip."

At this school, all teachers use behavioral clip charts as part of their classroom management routines. The charts have five color zones, with blue representing excellent behavior, followed by green, yellow, orange, and red. Red results in a meeting with the principal and a phone call home to the family. Oliver frowns and slowly gets up from his desk, walks across the classroom to the clip chart on the wall, and moves a clip with his name on it from the yellow area to the orange zone. He trudges back to his desk, slumps in his seat, and keeps his eyes down throughout the rest of reading time.

Then it's time for social studies, and Ms. Ramirez begins calling on students to share the presentations they have been working on: the jobs they are interested in pursuing when they grow up. Tyler gets called on, and Oliver mutters, "Go do your stupid presentation now."

Jacob overhears. "Ms. Ramirez! Oliver just called Tyler stupid," he reports.

Oliver's clip lands in the red zone, and Ms. Ramirez places a quick call to the front office. A few moments later, Oliver storms out of the classroom and stomps his way to the office. As school policy requires, there will be a meeting with the principal and a call home to his parents.

———————

Let's think about this scenario a bit. Obviously, classroom management by clip chart is part of the problem. If the threat of humiliation were an effective way to encourage positive behaviors and discourage problematic ones, Oliver would not have been playing with his Pokémon cards in the first place. In addition, use of the clip chart has led some students, like Tyler and Jacob, to police their peers, which is not a behavior you'll find in supportive classrooms that build positive social and emotional skills.

Notice, too, that Oliver did not have a chance to deal with his emotional response to being caught breaking the rules. He was angry and perhaps embarrassed, but Ms. Ramirez missed an opportunity to label those emotions, help Oliver understand his natural reactions, and then support him to regulate his response. Over time, if Oliver continues to be punished for his negative emotional reactions, he'll learn to repress those feelings in the moment and take them out on others at a later time.

As we noted in Chapter 1, all teachers integrate social and emotional learning (SEL) into their classroom lessons, whether they are aware of doing so or not. One of the most impactful ways they do this is through their interactions with students, and as this scenario illustrates, the lessons students take away are not always positive or constructive ones. Consider:

- Oliver learned that his emotional responses of anger or embarrassment are not acceptable—and that maybe *he's* not acceptable either. He has also learned that he needs to express his anger toward Tyler under circumstances in which he won't get caught.
- Tyler learned that policing other's harmless behavior is acceptable. He may also be a bit worried about whether Oliver will seek revenge. With no established model for working out this kind of peer conflict in class,

Tyler will have to figure out how to protect himself during afternoon recess.

- The rest of the students learned less about Tyler's presentation than they might have, because they were distracted by the fact that Oliver was sent to the principal's office. They also learned that tattling and avoiding getting caught are valuable social tools in this classroom.

We share this story precisely because it is so *ordinary*. Little dramas like this play out every day in classrooms, under the radar, because teachers aren't accustomed to seeing incidents like this as evidence that their students need help developing emotional regulation skills. They might see Ms. Ramirez's classroom management strategies as subpar and sending a child to the principal's office for such a minor infraction as unnecessary. They might note that it will undermine her authority. But what we want everyone to focus on is the teaching opportunity Ms. Ramirez missed. Instead of what she did do, she could have

- Redirected Oliver's attention and returned to the lesson.
- Helped Oliver label his emotion ("It seems like you're feeling upset right now. Can you tell me about it?").
- Prompted Oliver to use a self-soothing technique ("Three deep breaths to clear your head").
- Spoke privately to Tyler later ("What might be a better way to help your friend Oliver when you see he is distracted?").

The practical reason to carefully attend to the emotional climate of a classroom is because emotion has the power to enhance or inhibit learning. It's an established aspect of sound pedagogy, contributing to memory formation (Phelps, 2004) and positively affecting student engagement (Naragon-Gainey, McMahon, & Chacko, 2017). Teachers can use emotion to capture and keep attention (Öhman, Flykt, & Esteves, 2001). When establishing a direction for learning at the beginning of a lesson, we can identify what about the upcoming content will resonate with our students (Fisher & Frey, 2011). We can also use emotion to our advantage when we express warmth and caring toward our students, create a calm and orderly environment for learning, get excited by a topic we're teaching, or joke and laugh with our students. You might even think about the instructional strategies we use as attempts to influence the emotions of students in a way that will enhance their learning.

Now think of what teachers might accomplish if we let our students in on all of this—if we deliberately built our students' knowledge of self and their awareness of the role that their emotions play in everything they do, including learning. In this chapter, we discuss foundational principles of emotional processes and their vital role in learning, and explore some of the critical components of emotional regulation that teachers can help students develop.

Emotional Regulation Defined

What do you do when you are frustrated, or worried, or bored? Chances are very good that you have acquired a host of responses to these emotions—responses that are socially acceptable. If they weren't socially acceptable, you might not have any friends or be able to hold a job; you might even be in prison. These responses also enhance your quality of life. Knowing how to cope with frustration and cheer yourself up in healthy ways is vital for maintaining stability. Regaining calm when you're feeling anxious is essential for maintaining balance. All of these are examples of emotional self-regulation, which involves a complex set of skills considered vital for adult success.

Emotional self-regulation in school-age children is now fairly well-understood as a set of skills that can be taught. To be sure, personality characteristics, as well as developmental factors and individual experiences, influence children's ability to regulate their emotions. But we can teach them how to identify, respond to, and manage their own emotional states, which helps them to establish and maintain relationships (see Chapter 5). Critically, children's ability to regulate their emotions influences how they are perceived by peers and adults (Argyle & Lu, 1990; Furr & Funder, 1998). This has clear ramifications for classroom learning.

Let's return to the chapter's opening scenario for a moment. Ms. Ramirez might attribute Oliver's name-calling and angry classroom exit to negative character traits and a lack of maturity. Tyler's tattling probably didn't win him many admirers, either, and his classmates might decide he's untrustworthy and should be avoided. Both Oliver and Tyler might have responded differently if they were equipped with more tools to regulate their emotions. The entire exchange might not have occurred had these students experienced a strong SEL curriculum replete with attention to emotional regulation.

The work of teaching emotional regulation begins with fostering habits of reflection, self-checking, and response moderation. Children need to understand that emotions are normal and natural, that some emotions feel better or worse than others, and that some emotions make us feel out of control. We might *hit the ceiling, go ballistic, fly off the handle.* Notice the violence of these descriptions. It's important for children to understand that they don't have to be governed by negative emotions, and the first step is to help students accurately label their feelings.

Identifying Emotions

A lot of being human is seeking to understand the emotions of others, and this work gets underway almost immediately. Infants read faces and interpret the emotions of their parents and caregivers. They check for other facial expressions and body movements and mirror them in their own gestures. Toddlers struggle to link language to emotions, and the "terrible twos" can be understood in part as the lack of expressive language to properly convey feelings. Adults help young children build this vocabulary by providing labels. "I can see you're feeling afraid right now," we tell them when they awaken from a nightmare. Then we hold them, sing to them, and distract them with a story until they are settled. In doing so, we are providing instruction on how to manage emotions.

As the lives of children entering school become more complex, their emotional management task does, too. Students in the primary grades are challenged to manage their emotions in large groups of other children, away from the support of their caregivers. In these environments, cues that help students label their emotions can be very valuable. Some teachers use posters that feature different facial expressions and accompanying labels to help a child who is struggling to express what he or she is feeling. First grade teacher

Wes Logan uses a chart like this when talking with his students. "I use it regularly in class to build their self-awareness," he explained. "Sometimes I use it to talk about my own emotions, like after the principal visits our class. I explain to them that I was excited, but I was also a little anxious."

Mr. Logan carries this approach over to the content side as well. "We label the emotions of the characters we encounter in stories," he told us. "It's a way to understand them." As part of a social studies unit on the occupations of people in the community, his class discusses the emotional aspect of different jobs. "We talk about how police officers must feel scared sometimes, and how a store owner might get frustrated when she's asked the same questions by her customers. This opens up the discussion of how these professionals recognize and handle their feelings."

Seventh grade English teacher Lydia Navarro has a "word wall" of emotion terminology in her classroom, and she uses it to expand academic vocabulary while building her students' ability to identify emotional states. "I introduce words in the context of writing," she explained. "Finding the 'just right' word to explain a character's inner life is a mark of a great writer. Throughout the year, we collect terms we encounter and cluster them together to be able to show relationships." At the start of every school year, Ms. Navarro introduces the concept of clustering terms on a continuum using a process called *shades of meaning*. She models how terms can be used to describe a range of related emotions, using paint chips donated by a local hardware store. "The paint chips are a visual representation of shades of color. We began by collecting terms that serve as intensifiers," she told us. With this foundation established, she teaches students about the wheel of emotions (Plutchik, 1997; see Figure 3.1), with its eight basic feelings: joy, trust, fear, surprise, sadness, disgust, anger, and anticipation. The intersection of these basic feelings produces other secondary emotions:

- Joy + trust = love
- Trust + fear = submission
- Fear + surprise = awe
- Surprise + sadness = disapproval
- Sadness + disgust = remorse

- Disgust + anger = contempt
- Anger + anticipation = aggressiveness
- Anticipation + joy = optimism

"We use the wheel as a guide for how to properly convey the right emotion to explain a feeling, and we add terms we encounter in our readings," Ms. Navarro explained. "We've added the words *tenderness, stunned, suspicious*, and *elated* just this week." And she stressed that it's more than just knowing the dictionary definition of a word; "it's properly positioning these emotions in context. The class decided that *tenderness* belonged with love, while *stunned* was linked to awe. There's a precision they are gaining in understanding their emotions and those of others."

Emotional Self-Perception

Jones and colleagues note that "children must learn to recognize, express, and regulate their emotions before they can be expected to interact with others who are engaged in the same set of processes" (2017, p. 16). Being able to recognize emotions is more than simply having labels—students need to learn to apply those labels accurately to themselves and others. The ability to do this develops through practice, especially when that practice includes having lots of opportunities to check their emotional state and talk about what they and others are feeling.

Teachers have the power to make emotional check-ins a routine within the classroom. The middle school teachers at the school where we work start the year with the film *Inside Out* (Rivera & Docter, 2015) to establish a common vocabulary of emotions. The characters—Joy, Anger, Fear, Disgust, and Sadness—are drawn from Plutchik's work on emotions and are expressed by Riley, a girl who is in conflict after moving to a new city. At our school, each student desk contains a small visual representation of the range of emotions discussed in the movie, and students are asked at various times during the week to note their present state. This is done silently, and although students will sometimes write about how they are feeling, more often they do not.

FIGURE 3.1
Plutchik's Wheel of Emotions

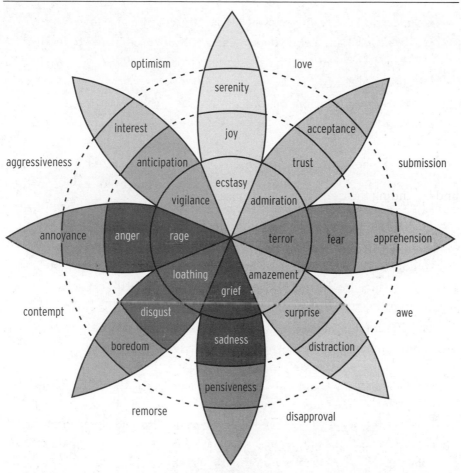

Source: Adapted from Plutchik-wheel.svg by Machine Elf 1735. Retrieved from Wikimedia Commons, https://commons.wikimedia.org/w/index.php?curid=13285286

However, these check-ins become a habit over time. Grace, a 7th grader, told us, "I've gotten better at checking in with myself. Like if I'm bored, I have to notice it and do something about it."

Teachers of younger children might regularly ask them to stop and notice their feelings, and then use colors to describe what those feelings are. The

Zones of Regulation model (Kuypers, 2013) provides a helpful, color-based vocabulary for expressing emotional states:

- *Blue zone:* I am feeling sad, sick, tired, bored, moving slowly
- *Green zone:* I am feeling happy, calm, OK, focused, ready to learn
- *Yellow zone:* I am feeling frustrated, worried, silly/wiggly, excited, a little out of control
- *Red zone:* I am feeling mad/angry, terrified, yelling/hitting, elated, out of control

Unlike the behavior clip chart used by Ms. Ramirez in our opening scenario, these color zones are not punitive. Using this technique described by Kuypers (2013), children learn that everybody has feelings, all feelings are acceptable, and knowing what you are feeling can help you figure out how to respond to that feeling. Feelings are clustered according to levels of "alertness" (akin to levels of intensity) rather than external judgments of "good" and "bad" (which by themselves do little to build children's capacity to manage their emotions).

Third grade teacher Asia Jackson-Phelps asks her students to check on their emotional state each morning as they arrive to class:

> I've got a magnetic board with each child's name listed. They put a magnet next to their name to tell me they are in attendance, and whether they will be ordering lunch. Last year I added a zone report. I've got colored magnets for each zone. It gives me a quick temperature check of the class, and I can tailor my language and responses to each of them.

Her students gain experience using this language as they encounter characters in their readings, which contributes to their comprehension of texts as well as to their understanding of others' emotional states. Recently, Ms. Jackson-Phelps has been reading aloud *Poppy* (Avi, 1995) after lunch every day, which has helped her students identify emotions:

> There's a point in the story where Poppy, the field mouse, realizes that Mr. Orax, the barn owl, has been ruling over them using lies and fear. Poppy is

figuring out what to do with this new information. One of the students said, "She's in the yellow zone now!" I wanted to stay with that idea, so I asked more questions about it. We talked about how being excited can easily become a loss of control. They made some predictions about what Poppy might do if she didn't watch out—like her excitement might make her take a foolish chance. It was completely consistent with the story, but it was also a moment when they got to think through what the possible consequences could be, depending on how Poppy regulated her emotions.

Students who are adept at emotional self-regulation can accurately perceive their current emotional state, anticipate how they will feel throughout the rest of day, and take steps to maintain their equilibrium. Brackett and Frank (2017) advise providing older students with opportunities to gauge how their emotional state changes in different settings. Here are four questions they suggest asking to spark self-reflection and discussion:

1. How do you feel at the start of the school day?
2. What emotions do you feel throughout the day while learning?
3. Do you feel differently when walking in the hallway, sitting in the lunchroom, or at recess or passing period?
4. How do you feel at the end of the school day?

That third question is especially interesting if you work with adolescents, as we do. We often find ourselves talking with a student out in the hallway while class is going on. It is surprising how often the student will ask us to escort them back into the room because he or she doesn't want to walk in front of the class. When asked why, they usually tell us that it is because they feel self-conscious and uncomfortable. "Everyone will watch me," they say. As adults, we are sometimes unaware of the specific anxieties of adolescents. It is a reminder that asking questions about their emotional states is an opportunity for us to learn more about them, too.

Ninth grade science teacher Ellery Davis introduces a method for anticipating emotions during the first week of school as part of a schoolwide Welcome Week. "Ninth graders are super-nervous being at the high school," he said. "You can see the fear in their eyes." He uses the online planner feature of the school's learning management system, which has been customized to include an emotions planner. Mr. Davis and his students discuss times that are likely to provoke heightened emotions, such as taking a test, presenting to the class, completing labs with people you don't know well, and contributing to class discussions. After listing anxiety-provoking conditions likely to occur in his science class, they discuss ways to plan for these situations. "The list usually begins with things they can do to calm themselves, such as breathing and stretching," he said. "Then we start digging deeper. How can you reduce anxiety before a test? Study and preparation help."

Mr. Davis's third period students listed a variety of methods suitable for different situations, including getting a drink of water, identifying a good study partner, writing a to-do checklist, and finding the best place to sit during labs. "A big one is getting enough sleep. Teenagers are really bad at this, so I do a lesson on the biological effects of rest and its relationship to stress." He also has become a fan of fidget toys and stress balls. "I don't find them to be much of a distraction. There's some novelty for the first few days, but they become a part of the classroom materials pretty quickly. A few rules need to be reviewed, but that's about it."

Impulse Control and Delayed Gratification

We intentionally held these two topics until later in this chapter, because without an understanding of emotional self-regulation, the subject quickly becomes a discussion about external control. Children's ability to control impulses and delay gratification, like other elements of emotional regulation, is influenced by personality, experiences, and developmental factors. Not surprisingly, older students are better at both than younger ones, and if you teach older students, they may come to you with some strategies already in place. The teacher's role here is to pull the emotional work of impulse control and delaying gratification forward, explain and discuss these skills, and support students' efforts to develop and deploy them. This can be complicated work, so we'll look at each of these related topics one at a time.

Impulse Control

"Look before you leap." That's one we heard a lot growing up.

"Stop and think," we remind students who seem ready to react in an instant.

"Pump the brakes," we hear students tell one another.

All of these pieces of advice are appropriate when somebody's about to do something rash. Notice that all of them urge a pause, a moment of reflection —time to consider and chose a deliberate action instead of automatically engaging in a reaction.

Although impulses seem to arise out of nowhere, they're always a reaction to a stimulus, and often that stimulus is emotional: anger, boredom, confusion, anxiety, and so on. The key to impulse control, then, is being able to identify the triggering mechanism and being ready to act in a different way when that wire is tripped. For example, once a student recognizes that feelings of anger or fear will make him more likely to lash out physically, he can make a plan for what he'll do next time he gets angry—count to 10, take a deep breath, talk to a trusted adult, or remove himself from the classroom to get away from whatever is feeding his anger.

This last example underscores why it's so beneficial to know emotional regulation strategies and help students develop their "Plan Bs." Think of how many teachers would see an angry student's choice to leave the classroom as defiance rather than impulse control—as walking out rather than walking away. We need to provide our students with various means of regulating their emotions, and if we don't include "escape" as an option, we rob them of a valuable tool.

Classrooms structured to teach students impulse control around "hot" emotions like anger and fear include spaces for children to retreat. These places should be inviting and somewhat distanced from the thick of the action. Whereas older elementary students can often calm themselves by sitting in a comfortable chair in a corner, younger children might need a bit more physical sheltering, such as a small tent or a bean bag chair they can sink down into, with a small blanket to use as a shield. These spaces should never be used as punishment destinations; they must remain a safe place for retreat. That said, there's nothing wrong with inviting students to make use of these spaces when you see signs of agitation, labeling the emotion for them as you do so: "You're frustrated because of what happened when we lined up for recess. Do you want to use the chill-out chair so you can collect your thoughts?"

It's also smart to establish set procedures for middle and high school students to self-initiate a break when they need to. We know there are lots of rules in schools about who can be out of class—you need permission, you need a pass, and so on. But a student who is trying to manage the impulse to say something insulting to another classmate after a personal disagreement really may need to remove herself physically from the environment. We have written about a process used at the school where we teach, affectionately called TLC (Fisher, Frey, & Pumpian, 2012). A small table and two chairs are set up in a hallway nook. A sign taped to the table says, "How can I help? I have the time." Adult staff members hang out at the TLC table (it's a great way to catch up on e-mail without being holed up in an office). Anyone can sit in the empty chair—sometimes it's another adult—to have a conversation. Students who are on an assigned or self-initiated break can use this opportunity to talk with someone who is ready to help.

A second key to better impulse control is careful listening. Good listeners are able to more accurately understand the context, tone, and intent of another person's message. How often is conflict the result of poorly delivered and understood messages? Of jumping to conclusions about others' meaning or intentions? A simple way to support listening skill development is to regularly ask students to repeat or rephrase a direction. (This has the added benefit of installing the habit of pausing to think a direction all the way through.) Listening games for young children, like Red Light/Green Light; Simon Says; and Head, Shoulders, Knees, and Toes, also foster careful listening.

Eighth grade social studies teacher Allan Sabah uses barrier games in his class to develop his students' ability to listen well. Students work in pairs, but they are seated back to back so they cannot see what the other is doing. One student has a simple visual drawing related to the unit of study (e.g., a flag, a map, a political symbol). The other student has paper and pen, but cannot see the object. The goal is for the team to reproduce the original visual as closely as possible, without naming the object. "So a student who has a picture of the Union Jack flag used during the Revolutionary War needs to give directions about drawing a rectangle, creating a red cross in the middle, and so on," Mr. Sabha explained. "Map outlines are harder, so it really pushes their communication and listening skills." Although students do this as a fun activity, there's content and emotional regulation learning going on. "They get better at predicting what the object they are drawing might be, based on the context of the unit. We also talk about how clear two-way communication is necessary to achieve the goal."

 WHEN STUDENTS NEED MORE SUPPORT . . .

Some students need more individualized support to develop the capacity to modulate their impulses. Whether due to disability, trauma, or lack of experience, these students can quickly ruffle a teacher's feathers. Some students might be aggressive toward other children, or "overreact" in situations that provoke heightened emotions (e.g., throwing a tantrum in frustration, laughing too loudly and too long). Older students may appear argumentative, always angling for "the last word and the first turn," which is how one parent we know described his own child. The outward behaviors of a child with poor impulse control can be wrongly interpreted as evidence of the child's character and parenting rather than executive function in need of development.

As noted, all students with reduced impulse control can benefit from understanding what their triggers are, but we'd like to dig into to the concept a little more here. Behavior of any kind is a response to something, with the goal being to gain or avoid something else. These are the ABCs of behavior: antecedents, behavior, and consequences. *Antecedents* are those people, events, or environmental cues that occur before the behavior. Some are fast triggers, meaning that they happen immediately before the behavior; others are slow triggers, occurring minutes, hours, or days before the behavior. An example of a fast trigger is one student muttering something offensive under his breath, and another student slapping him in the face. Hitting a student is a problematic behavior that must be addressed, but we also have to address what precipitated it. On the other hand, a slow trigger might contribute to the same behavior. Perhaps a student had a restless night as his parents argued for hours, and then when he went downstairs in the morning to fix breakfast, his mother announced that his father had left the family, running back into her room in tears. The boy left for school without eating, sulked silently through his morning classes, then navigated the crowded school hallway leading to the cafeteria. He is accidentally jostled by a bigger student and strikes the other boy in retaliation. Again, the problematic behavior must be addressed. But to only focus on the fast trigger (the jostle) without also examining the slow triggers (his frustration, anxiety, lack of sleep, lack of food) would be to do a great disservice to a student in need of emotional support.

These two examples are not in and of themselves signs of an impulse control disorder, although a pattern of such behaviors might be. When that is the case, helping the student identify slow and fast triggers can be helpful. When Leland, whose father was away from the family due to a military deployment, started exhibiting signs of reduced impulse control, his 9th grade teachers were concerned. He was quick to anger, even when the problem was a minor one. He was physically more agitated, tipping back his chair (and falling a few times), frequently out of his seat when he shouldn't be, and requesting to leave class more often. Leland's teachers met with him to figure things out. With help from his teachers and the school counselor, Leland collected data on himself about triggers, noting what conditions were occurring on good days and on bad days. In time, he noticed that lack of sleep took a toll. He started arriving at school earlier so he could get breakfast and settle himself a bit before the school day. Although there was no instant fix (Leland's home life remains complicated), he acquired a bit more knowledge about himself and learned to manage the triggers he could control.

The patterns that exist within the consequences are also worth examining. In behavior analysis, a *consequence* is simply the result of the behavior. Consequences can be understood as four functions of the behavior: social attention, avoidance or escape, obtaining an item, and power or control. All of these functions play a role in everyday life, and for the most part, we have figured out how to achieve these goals. We use these functions each and every day. The difference is in how we enact these functions. Figure

3.2 contrasts a set of examples from adult lives for each function: one that is socially acceptable, and one that is socially problematic. As you see, the routes chosen to achieve the same consequence can vary dramatically—from positive to negative and even to illegal.

FIGURE 3.2
Socially Acceptable and Unacceptable Adult Behaviors for Various Consequences

Consequence	Socially Acceptable Behavior	Socially Unacceptable Behavior
Social attention	You greet colleagues with a smile and a cheerful "Good morning!" and they greet you back.	You insult your colleagues, and when they react angrily, you say, "Can't you take a joke?"
Avoidance or escape	You politely excuse yourself from a tedious meeting so you can take a short break and stretch your legs.	You loudly exclaim at a meeting, "Oh my gosh, this is so boring! Can't you please just shut up?"
Obtaining an item	You pay for your purchase at the coffee shop.	You grab a protein bar on display at the coffee shop and leave without paying.
Power or control	You write a customer review of a product that was a disappointment.	You write a note demanding a refund, then tie it to a brick and heave it through the store window.

Children and adolescents with poor impulse control sometimes have a more limited repertoire for achieving their goals. They rely on behaviors that are the most efficient way to obtain what they want; social acceptability often doesn't enter into the equation.

Pattern analysis is useful for examining consequences to problematic impulsive behavior. A student who is constantly calling out in class may be seeking social attention. The girl who asks to go to the restroom at inopportune times may be doing so to avoid a difficult academic task. The small child who grabs materials from others may lack the communication skills to ask for what she wants. The teenager who says, "Stop talking to me!" when you ask him to move to another seat might be seeking power, more concerned about looking tough in front of his friends than complying with your request. Understanding the possible function of a behavior can provide insight to the student about his intentions, and help the student build other skills that can replace the problematic one.

For example, the boy who calls out answers rather than raise his hand might benefit from working with you to set a goal for reducing this behavior. You need to reinforce when he does raise his hand by consistently calling on him so that he learns that he can gain your attention without worry. The girl who escapes to the restroom could benefit from developing some help-seeking strategies so that she doesn't need to flee quite so often. The small child who grabs materials from others needs skills development in making requests verbally.

The last function of behavior, seeking power and control, can be the most difficult to address because it is rooted in fear. Among all emotions, fear is significant because it is about self-preservation. There is a growing body of evidence that children and adolescents with attention and impulse control problems have "difficulty processing threat-related emotion" (Flegenheimer, Lugo-Candelas, Harvey, & McDermott, 2018, p. 336). The adolescent who postures in front of his peers by refusing to follow your request is motivated by fear of losing his social standing. First and foremost, he needs you to be calm and nonthreatening in order not to escalate the situation. In the long term, you can adjust the environment a bit to ensure that he has choices (real ones, not "or else" threats), such as selecting the independent reading book from a list you've provided him. Another environmental change is to make your content instruction relevant to his interests. Most effective of all is to build a relationship with this student, modeling for him positive social and emotional skills. In doing so, you help him see that you and the school environment are not a threat to him.

Abrupt changes or significant delays in impulse control can signal more serious concerns. It should come as no surprise that children and adolescents who experience traumatic events exhibit poorer impulse control compared to same-age peers (Danese & McEwen, 2012). Adverse childhood experiences themselves cluster into three domains: childhood maltreatment, family dysfunction, and social disadvantage. Students who show a marked change in impulse control may very well be experiencing trauma, which merits investigation and intervention—and teachers are on the front line for noticing when such changes occur.

Delayed Gratification

Mention "delayed gratification," and most educators will think about marshmallows—more specifically, about the seminal set of studies that were conducted with children between the ages of 4 and 6 by Walter Mischel at Stanford University. The children were offered a marshmallow or other treat and told they could eat it immediately, but that if they waited 15 minutes, they could have two treats. The researcher then left the child alone in the room with the marshmallow. Some ate the treat as soon as the researcher left, but many others worked at distracting themselves for long enough to get the promised two marshmallows. The children used a variety of techniques, including talking to themselves and turning their chairs so they couldn't see the marshmallow. As expected, the ability to delay gratification correlated to the age of the children. But what weren't expected were the findings in a series of longitudinal studies on participants, now adults. Those who were successful at waiting to eat two treats had higher SAT scores and more active prefrontal cortex activity than those who were not able to delay gratification (Casey et al., 2011; Shoda, Mischel, & Peake, 1990).

Teachers help students develop a stronger ability to delay gratification by setting *reasonable and attainable* classroom goals that result in a reward. If the reward is too far in the future compared to the children's age, it is likely to fail. For instance, having a reward that is set for the last day of the school year is not reasonable for kindergartners. A year to them represents 20 percent of the time they have been alive! An end-of-day reward is much more reasonable for 5-year-olds. Basing a reward on the expectation that every student in the class will need to earn a perfect score on a test may not be attainable. But raising the class average for the next chemistry test might be. Setting impossible goals for students does not motivate them. Some teachers use a visual such as a jar of marbles or a thermometer so that students can see their gains accumulating.

Second grade teacher Karen Franklin is an avowed sports fan, and her classroom is filled with sports-related items from the local professional and college teams. In keeping with her interests, she has set up an electronic scoreboard that allows students to see how their performance contributes to class rewards. "I award table points for prosocial behaviors such as helping tablemates, completing tasks, and being attentive and kind," she said.

> I started the year with short-term rewards for the end of the day. But as the year has gone on, I've been increasing the amount of time they need to reach a goal. For example, we have Fresh Fruit Friday each time the class has reached 10,000 points.

Mrs. Franklin told us it usually takes the class two or three weeks to rack up 10,000 points. "We have a big goal on the table now: 100,000 class points, and then we'll take a field study trip to a destination of their choice." She explained that when the class reaches the goal, they'll come to consensus on where to go. She also pointed out that the activity helps to reinforce students' number sense about large numbers, which is one of their mathematics content goals.

The original marshmallow studies did not test the possible effect environment plays in children's ability to delay gratification. More recently, a team of researchers wondered whether there would be a negative effect when the adult did not reliably keep a promise. They replicated the original study with 3-year-olds, but with one key difference: some children had a prior experience with the adult researcher where a promise of art supplies wasn't kept. When the children were later given the choice of delaying the marshmallow reward, those who had been in the unreliable environment lasted an average of only three minutes before eating it. Those who had been in a reliable environment waited an average of 12 minutes, which is a monumental amount of time for a toddler to wait for anything (Kidd, Palmeri, & Aslin, 2013). This is an important reminder that we need to be scrupulously consistent and reliable for our students. Learning to delay gratification is dependent on being able to trust the world, and our classrooms should be a place where our word is as good as gold.

Stress Management

Feelings of stress are a physiological response to the environment. Heart rate increases, breathing quickens, and adrenaline is released. Although stress is typically associated with negative conditions, it's more accurate to specify that there are two types of stress: eustress and distress. *Eustress* is "good stress." It's what gets you up in the morning and positively affects motivation, performance, and well-being. *Distress*, on the other hand, has a negative effect on motivation, performance, and well-being.

Stressed students (by which we really mean *distressed* students, but we'll use the vernacular from now on) perform worse, forget more of what they have learned, and actively avoid thinking about the content outside the classroom. Ramirez, McDonough, and Ling (2017), who studied mathematics classrooms, sum up their findings quite bluntly: "Classroom stress promotes motivated forgetting of mathematics knowledge" (p. 812). Even worse, high levels of distress at the time of learning are associated with a lower capacity to take in new information (Vogel & Schwabe, 2016).

Students need to be taught techniques for recognizing and managing their stress levels. One recommendation is simply for students to learn to think positive thoughts and to "choose their attitude." That might sound soft, but it's been tried in a lot of classrooms and seems to work. For example, when Lexi Salazar talks with her 2nd grade students, they rehearse positive thoughts such as "I am a good friend. I like learning. We have pride in our classroom." According to Ms. Salazar, these brief experiences help build students' confidence in themselves and lower stress. Simple breathing techniques can also help quiet nerves and focus attention. "One technique I teach them is bumblebee breathing," she explained. "They close their eyes and take a deep breath in, then exhale slowly through their mouths, humming softly like a bee. We do this a few times and then get to work."

In Samantha Aguirre's class, students engage in postural feedback before any stressful or anxiety-provoking event. Cuddy (2015) found that people who assumed an expansive physical posture (e.g., arms up and spread apart) before completing a demanding task reported an improved self-perception of feelings of power. Cuddy hypothesized that this physical positioning, originally termed "power posing," triggered hormonal changes. While Cuddy has since retracted the claim about the effect on hormones, the original theory has borne out in a statistical analysis of 55 published studies (Cuddy, Schultz, & Fosse, 2018). We have seen students engage in postural feedback on their own to gain confidence and reduce their stress. If it helps a few students feel more confident and gets them out of their chair, pushing some extra oxygen to their brains, we're OK with it!

Of course, teachers should do more than just make positive affirmations and tell students to think positively. Creating an environment that reduces (or at least does not add to) students' stress levels is equally important. The physical environment should be neat and clutter-free, with careful attention given to the number of visual distractions in the room. Although it is valuable to post language charts, student work, and the like in the classroom, keep in mind that over the course of the school year, these things accumulate. Don't forget to take down items as new ones are put up.

Outside noise levels, although not fully under our control, can be reduced somewhat by the use of sound-reducing objects such as plants, upholstered couches, and rugs. In addition, make students aware of the noise they generate within the room and teach them ways to modulate the collective sound level. Third grade teacher Bella Sanchez uses a floor lamp with a dimmer switch to signal the relative sound level to her students. When the light is dim, the sound level for the activity should be low, such as when students are reading. A brighter light signals a higher acceptable sound level, such as when students are engaged in collaborative learning.

Adjusting a classroom's academic structure can also reduce stress. The use of practice tests, which are administered a week or so in advance of an exam, has a stress-reducing effect on students (Vogel & Schwabe, 2016). Practice tests are shorter versions of the actual test and are designed to highlight key skills and concepts. Although they are not graded, they are scored so that students can analyze their performance. Being able to accurately estimate their current knowledge compared to what will be expected at the time of the test can help eliminate stressful uncertainty and provide a reassuring direction for further study. A meta-analysis of practice tests showed that they are effective in both elementary and secondary settings, and that a single administration is sufficient; multiple practice tests on the same unit didn't have a greater impact on student learning (Adesope, Trevisan, & Sundararajan, 2017). It should be noted that the positive impact of practice tests is only realized if students are given the opportunity to analyze their results and plan how they will improve their learning.

Finally, raising student awareness of stress and its effect on learning can be of great value. Many SEL programs include specific lessons on stress management, which can be an effective way of introducing this topic to students. Jim Kennedy started a list called "Top Ten Things to Do When You're Feeling Stressed" in his 5th grade classroom, and students added techniques as they learned about them. "The first ones were mostly about breathing, stretching, that kind of thing," he said. "Over the year, they have added reminders like talking to me, a family member, or a friend when they are feeling stressed about their learning. It shows me that they are recognizing the network of support they have around them." Mr. Kennedy models this himself, taking advantage of times when he needs to breathe or stretch in order to relieve stress, and thinking aloud about the experience as he does it.

Coping

In Chapter 2 we discussed resiliency as a necessary mindset to foster in students. Resiliency may be an attitude, but it does not exist in a vacuum. There is an emotional component to resiliency, and that involves using coping skills.

Mechanisms for coping include those related to stress management and controlling anxiety. The intersection of coping and emotional regulation is relatively new, and some techniques fall into the realm of cognitive regulation, which is the focus of Chapter 4. Cognitive regulatory techniques for coping include solving problems and seeking help and social support. Emotional regulation techniques include acceptance of a situation, distraction, and stopping negative "doomsday" thinking. A challenge in addressing the emotional aspect of coping is that it can look like problem behaviors related to poor impulse control. Emotion-focused coping skills include "seeking social support and escape/avoidance" (Compas et al., 2017, p. 941). In other words, coping can be adaptive (useful) or maladaptive (harmful). Maladaptive coping skills include blaming one's self, blaming others, denial, and withdrawing from other people. However, adaptive coping skills can serve as protective factors for dealing with negative life events.

One particular category of adaptive coping skills for stress and anxiety management we'd like to discuss is called *distractors*. You may be familiar with distractors, as they are a common feature of SEL programs. Bethany O'Brien, a 6th grade math teacher, develops a list of healthy distractors her students can use in the classroom and outside school. Some of the distractors are targeted at altering one's physiological state: going for a bike ride, walking around the block, or drinking water. She has taught her students a number of finger exercises designed to increase hand and wrist flexibility. "I used to play piano, and my teacher had me do all these finger exercises for dexterity and strength," she explained. "But they're also really good for getting some blood flowing, and it gives students something else to think about."

The class also keeps a running list of mental distractors they can use. Some have been suggested by students: cuddling with a pet, reading a book, and listening to music. Ms. O'Brien keeps colored pencils and markers on a quiet table, with several adult coloring books scattered about. "I like the quiet table in particular because it gives my kids a chance to relocate without leaving the class. They can still be listening to the lesson but also just a little bit apart." Recently, she added human interaction to the list. "We've made lists of the people in our lives we can talk to," Ms. O'Brien told us. "Parents, friends, siblings, me . . . at this age, sometimes it's just that reminder that there are people around them who care about them that makes the difference."

Sometimes the best person to talk to is oneself. Eleventh grade English teacher Samuel Ito teaches his students about Aristotle and the ancient Greek origin of the word *catharsis*: "I first introduce it in the dramatic context, as comedy and tragedy in theater is supposed to have a cathartic effect on the audience." He then introduces another means of cathartic release to cope with stress and anxiety: "Journal writing. I show them a photo of 23 years of personal journals I have on a bookshelf at home," he said. Mr. Ito keeps blank journals he picks up at a local thrift shop to give to students who might be interested, and is exploring the use of journaling mobile applications. Such apps are password-protected—"better than a diary with a key"—and can include photos and videos.

Takeaways

Emotions influence learning and behavior. Much like a speed governor on a diesel engine, they regulate the speed at which information and experiences are processed. However, when emotions run too hot, the brain and body can quickly become overloaded. Children need to learn about their emotions and how to accurately name and recognize them. Emotions play a distinctive role in contributing to a student's impulse control and ability to delay gratification, and some students need more intensive supports to develop their capacity to do so. Stress and anxiety can be debilitating if unchecked, so students need to acquire a toolkit of coping mechanisms. However, simply telling students about emotional regulation is not enough to help them develop those skills. It is crucial that we examine and restructure our classrooms and schools to better support emotional self-regulation.

QUESTIONS FOR REFLECTION

1. When and where do your students learn about how to identify and label emotions in themselves and others? How can you expand the emotional vocabulary of your students?
2. In what ways could you integrate emotional self-regulation into your content?
3. What systems exist in your school and district to support students who need more guidance with developing better impulse control?
4. Where can you find resources that will help you create opportunities to extend your students' ability to delay gratification?
5. What are the signs you watch for to monitor your students' level of stress? How do you respond when you see or hear these signals? Ask a colleague to do an environmental scan of your classroom for physical

and aural elements that might contribute to higher levels of stress for your students.

6. What adaptive and maladaptive coping skills do you observe your students using?

CHAPTER 4

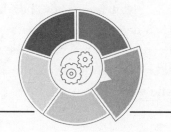

Cognitive Regulation

Metacognition | Attention | Goal setting
Recognizing & resolving problems | Help seeking
Decision making | Organizational skills

Third grader Finn shifts excitedly in his seat. In a few minutes, he's going to give a multimedia report he's been working on for an entire month. The assignment for him and his classmates in their dual immersion school? To prepare and present a report on a country of their choice in their second language—a seemingly tall order for these small boys and girls.

Finn had researched and prepared a presentation on Costa Rica. As he waited for class to start, he thought about the steps he'd taken.

Back when the assignment was first announced, he'd shared the teacher-provided schedule of due dates and tasks with his parents. He told them he wanted to have most of the work completed before spring break—which he would be spending at his grandparents' house. Because Finn realized he didn't know very much about the digital storytelling app he would use as a platform, he enlisted his older brother to show him some of the technical aspects of the program, such as how to embed a video. During an online research session in class, while searching for an image of the Costa Rican flag, he learned that the country would be holding a presidential election in a few days. Finn made a note in the online planning document his teacher set up to remind him to check on the results so that he could report the most current information about the country. Then, over the course of a few weeks, he and a peer partner had reviewed one another's developing presentations and given feedback. They had tweaked their presentations and practiced their deliveries to make sure they could complete them in five minutes. It had been hard to make sure the presentation wasn't too short or too long, Finn thought, but he felt confident in the work he'd done. He had learned a lot, and he was ready to share.

Finn's success was due in no small measure to his ability to cognitively regulate. He set a goal for himself (i.e., have the project mostly done by spring break), sought help, and used an organizational tool to keep track of progress. He didn't do it alone; Finn's teacher also played an important role in his project's success. But in many schools, planning, organizing, and creating are left up to the child (or the parents). Students who succeed in these circumstances tend to be viewed by their teachers as "capable," "motivated," or "mature," and their accomplishments are often attributed to character traits rather than explicit skill mastery.

Finn and his classmates were lucky to have a teacher who knew better. She created the conditions that would allow her students to learn and practice the skills of cognitive regulation by

- Developing a time line with interim check-ins to help students gauge their progress and chunking the assignment into smaller components.
- Modeling her thinking about approaching, planning, and completing a large task.
- Fostering a helping environment to support student decision making.
- Establishing work partnerships to encourage peer feedback.
- Communicating the project details to families so they could be engaged in the process.

In other words, Finn's teacher integrated principles of social and emotional learning (SEL), specifically cognitive self-regulation, into content instruction. As we have noted in previous chapters, when SEL is confined to a stand-alone program with little integration into the milieu of the classroom, attainment of program goals is reduced (Jones et al., 2017). In this chapter, we explore the

SEL competencies that most closely intersect with the academic instruction classroom teachers do each day, focusing on actions you can take to develop your students' cognitive regulation abilities.

Cognitive Regulation Defined

We have already explored emotional self-regulation, which has some similarities with cognitive self-regulation. *Self-regulated learning*, in general, refers to strategic, intentional, and metacognitive behavior, motivation, and cognition focused on a specific goal. "Students can be described as self-regulated to the degree that they are metacognitively, motivationally, and behaviorally active participants in their own learning process" (Zimmerman, 1989, p. 329). In other words, cognitive self-regulation requires that students engage in behaviors that help them learn. They assume increased responsibility for their learning and are active participants in the processes and strategies their teachers use.

Zimmerman (1989) also notes the value of specific strategies that self-regulated learners use. In his words, "self-regulated learning strategies are actions and processes directed at acquiring information or skill that involve agency, purpose, and instrumentality perceptions by learners. They include such methods as organizing and transforming information, self-consequating, seeking information, and rehearsing or using memory aids" (p. 329).

All cognitive regulation depends on a person's being aware of his or her cognitive processes. The skill of *metacognition,* then, is the logical place for us to start.

Metacognition

Research has revealed that children may begin to develop metacognitive knowledge as early as age 3 (Marulis, Palincsar, Berhenke, & Whitebread, 2016). Metacognition is commonly understood to be "thinking about one's thinking," but it's more completely understood as a three-part skill set: the ability to (1) recognize one's own and other people's thinking, (2) consider the actions needed to complete a task, and (3) identify the strategies one might use to carry out those actions. For instance, preschool children with rudimentary metacognition can answer questions about how they completed a jigsaw puzzle, tell you what might have made the task easier (e.g., if all the pieces were different colors or the same), and tell you what strategies they used to complete the task (e.g., look at the picture on the box, sort the pieces by color, assemble the border pieces first). This ability to monitor and direct cognitive processes is critical for every learner regardless of age, and it's closely associated with the development of expertise in all fields (Sternberg, 1998). Think of how metacognition factors into teaching proficiency, for example. It's what allows us to plan and monitor lessons and reflect on past lessons in order to "debug" future ones (Jiang, Ma, & Gao, 2016).

Metacognition can be explicitly fostered through instruction. One of the best-known techniques is reciprocal teaching, which provides readers with a protocol for planning, monitoring, and reflecting their understanding of a text (Palincsar & Brown, 1984). Groups of students read a text that has been segmented at interim points and pause at designated stopping points to discuss the passage in order to develop a shared sense of understanding. The protocol requires students to jointly (1) summarize what has been read, (2) ask each other questions, (3) provide clarifying information to benefit others, and (4) formulate predictions about the next text segment.

Reciprocal teaching has amassed an impressive record of success, and it is used with students as young as 2nd graders. Significantly, gains in reading comprehension associated with reciprocal teaching are attributable not to the content of the text read but to the metacognitive prompting conditions of the protocol. Hattie's (2009) meta-analysis of reciprocal teaching studies attributes an effect size of .74 on student learning, far above the .40 effect size of a year's progress in a year of schooling (see our discussion of effect sizes in Chapter 1). These numbers make a strong case that metacognition deserves to be taught. And instruction in metacognition is most effective when it's embedded within the classroom's regular academic flow.

Third grade teacher Juan Cortez integrates opportunities for his students to engage in metacognitive thinking. As part of his efforts, he models his own metacognitive processes. Mr. Cortez thinks aloud each day, sharing his reflections about the content students are learning. For example, during a read-aloud about a strained friendship, Mr. Cortez paused and said,

> I'm seeing that friends do kind things for each other. And I'm seeing that friends apologize when they hurt each other's feelings. I'm going to make a list of things I learn about friends in this book and then compare it to what I learn in this other book. And then I'm going to think about which of these things I do on my own.

Mr. Cortez also provides students with opportunities to engage in their own metacognitive thinking. A poster in his classroom list examples of metacognitive behaviors students can practice, including the following:

- Identify what you already know.
- Summarize what you have learned.
- Communicate your knowledge, skills, and abilities to others.
- Set goals and monitor your progress.
- Evaluate and revise your work.

Mr. Cortez gives each student a small "personal goals" notebook at the beginning of the year to record what they want to accomplish both inside and outside school, and to reflect on their learning. Madison, a student in Mr. Cortez's class, described writing in her notebook:

> I was thinking about my progress and I wanted to write it down so I don't forget. I had a goal to learn to solve problems with patterns. I wasn't so good at that, but today I did it. I made progress because I figured out the pattern, and I asked Mr. Cortez for another practice problem to see if I could do it again.

Here, we see Madison engaging in metacognitive thinking and becoming increasing self-regulated as she learns. Of course, she still needs her teacher to guide the learning and provide her with strategies, but she is assuming more responsibility for her own thinking and, as her eagerness to try out her solution demonstrates, becoming more motivated in the process.

Attention

Along with a growing capability to think about one's own thinking comes the capacity to direct one's thinking in order to change behavior. Attention is a prime example of such directed thinking, and its value in the classroom is obvious. As students move through school, they need to sustain attention over longer periods of time, and sometimes in conditions that they may find monotonous (e.g., teacher lectures, extended reading and writing tasks). The conventional wisdom holds that school-age students will generally maintain attention for 5 to 10 minutes, although it is important to note that relative attention is task dependent. Watch a child absorbed in an intrinsically motivated task sometime, and marvel at the singular devotion to the activity.

In truth, any person's sustained attention is punctuated with intermittent loss of focus. Things seem to pop into our minds out of nowhere, and then we're off-task or off-topic. The skill of maintaining attention, then, is not about extending one's attention span but rather about choosing to return to a task after attention has been lost. It includes noticing when attention has faded and having strategies to bring it back to full strength. These strategies can be as simple as writing a note about the thing that popped into your head and then returning to the task at hand, or taking a breath and refocusing.

Adults routinely use strategies to help sustain attention and effort. For example, when you have a task to complete, setting a timer can do wonders to help you focus. We often tell our own writing students about Anthony Trollope, a prolific author from the Victorian age. He would set a timer for 15 minutes and challenge himself to write 250 words during that time. Trollope would sustain this pace for three hours early each morning, then report to his job at the postal service. He credited adherence to this routine for the 49 novels he produced in 35 years (Trollope, 2014).

Of course, Trollope didn't face the insistent lure of handheld digital devices. Anyone who has stood in front of middle or high school students in the past decade is familiar with the battle educators must wage against their students' in-class smartphone use. Just how bad is it? Rosen (2017) reported on studies of adolescents' behavior during 15-minute timed study sessions, noting that the researchers were discouraged to find that the average amount of time spent engaged in actual study was less than 10 minutes. More than a third of dedicated study time was lost to social media and phone checks. This would be depressing if the same study didn't also find that when students knew they would have a one-minute "tech check" after each 15 minutes of study, they maintained their study attention at higher rates.

Let's think about what was going on here. For these adolescents, it wasn't really the technology—having a smartphone—that provided the distraction; it was internal anxiety, the fear of missing out. When they knew they *would* be able to check their phones, they felt less of a need to do so. In other words, changing the environmental conditions to reduce students' anxiety increased their attention.

This insight is an important one. Although we can't explicitly teach attention, teachers do have quite a bit of influence on the conditions that can either contribute to or detract from a learner's ability to attend. For example, a quiet environment facilitates test taking, reading, writing, and other academic tasks. We know that, but do our students? The only way to be sure is to teach them.

Sixth grade science teacher Yasmin Farhad infuses information about the biological influences on attention into lessons on the central nervous system. She instructs her students about how to create learning environments that work in their favor. "We talk about attention and how the brain functions, especially in the frontal and parietal cortexes," she said. "I extend this to their reading habits. We discuss whether it is a good idea to have music playing in your headphones when you're doing your science homework. They link this to what they are learning about the brain." For Ms. Farhad, learning about cognitive regulation is a natural fit in her science class, where students are learning about the social, physical, and biological world. "I intentionally look for ways they can apply scientific knowledge to enhance their self-knowledge. One concept everyone masters? There's no such thing as multitasking! And they can explain why it is biologically impossible."

Teachers' metacognition plays a role in student attention, too. Expert teachers are able to monitor their audience for signs of restlessness and loss of attention. Further, they do not personalize outward student behavior as a sign of disrespect or attribute loss of attention to a student's flawed character. Instead, they change the pace and the activity, often incorporating some physical movement and communication. Teachers of young students might announce these as "brain breaks" to "shake the sillies out." Teachers of older students might lead a breathing exercise to refocus attention or call for a short partner-talk activity.

Such pauses are universally understood to be excellent classroom management techniques, but you can and should also leverage them to build students' sense that they can learn to regulate their attention. Pairing such breaks with reminders about the purpose (i.e., "We're doing this so you can refocus your attention") helps students become more aware of the importance of monitoring their own state and taking action to change it when necessary.

For example, U.S. history teacher Yvonne Mason uses the Think-Pair-Square technique in her classroom to help students refocus their attention on learning. First, there is some quiet time to reflect on a question or topic; then students share their thoughts with a designated partner before each partnership joins another partnership to "square up" and share their thinking as a group of four. Ms. Mason notes, "These brief conversations allow students time to process the content and check their thinking with others. I've found they are able to attend to the content longer, learn more, and develop a skill or tool for paying attention." This three-part routine provides students with time and space to consider a complex idea, and it has the added benefit of peer accountability. The habit of thinking alone *and* in the company of others is a useful skill in school and in life, and builds stamina to stay with a problem rather than turn away from it when answers don't come easily.

Goal Setting

Have you heard someone describe a student as being "unmotivated"? Maybe you have heard someone describe *you* as unmotivated. Certainly you can come up with at least one occasion where you found yourself feeling unmotivated in the face of a task.

You probably had some really good reasons why you were unmotivated. (Nancy feels this way about learning hot yoga, something Doug is newly interested in.) But low motivation often comes down to a single fact: you didn't have any goals for the activity. Doug has tapped into personal goals for yoga that are attached to incremental improvement of the 26 positions he performs each session, and he's looking at this practice as a pathway to improve his running. Doug also has, in his yoga instructor, a model for how each position should be performed, and he monitors his steady improvement toward the goals he has set. Put simply, one's motivation, or lack thereof, is fueled in large part by one's goals.

This presents a challenge for educators, because unlike adults who can select to engage in certain activities while avoiding others, students are generally expected to engage in all the tasks we set for them. They have to be in school all day and participate in classes whether or not they find those classes particularly interesting. Because motivation is variable and influenced by one's goals, those who hope to foster academic motivation must help students establish and monitor goals for academic learning.

But when it comes to influencing learning, not all academic goals are created equal. Let's take a closer look at the differences between performance goals and mastery goals.

Performance Goals

Some goals are about a student's standing relative to others rather than learning for learning's sake. These *performance goals* often have a social comparison element, because they can involve comparing one's performance against the performance of others. A good example of a performance goal is having a 4.0 grade point average (GPA). Certainly a student who sets this goal is likely to work hard to achieve it for several good reasons; perhaps she wants to be class valedictorian, she understands that class ranking influences college admission, and she knows her parents value exemplary grades. But pursuit of performance goals can come at a cost. A tight competition for the top ranking might mean giving up orchestra class in favor of a weighted advanced placement (AP) class.

This was the dilemma Nancy's daughter faced when she was a high school senior. At the end of her junior year, she and another student were tied for the top GPA. She had calculated that she needed to take a certain number of AP classes in order to be named valedictorian, but doing so would mean that she would not be able to take a fourth year of orchestra, an unweighted course that she loved. Ultimately, Nancy's daughter decided to remain in orchestra and finished the year as salutatorian without regrets. She later said, "It kept me playing violin during a really busy time in my life. I got an additional year to get better at it." Nancy's daughter got into a good college, played in one of the university orchestras ("the one for fun, not competition"), and earned a degree in computer sciences.

Performance goals are not inherently bad, and neither is having a performance goal orientation. It's actually very human—reflecting a natural desire for accomplishment, recognition, and esteem. But when a learner's goals are primarily of a performance nature, it can actually undermine learning. Performance goal–oriented students demonstrate higher levels of anxiety, in part because they worry about "looking smart" and not being perceived as "stupid." At its worst, a performance goal orientation can inhibit risk taking. How many of us have encountered a student who chooses to take a less challenging course because he sees it as a guaranteed *A* rather than stretch his abilities in a more difficult course? This is an example of a *performance-avoidance goal*, in that the student is trying to avoid performing more poorly than other classmates in the more challenging course.

Mastery Goals

Unlike performance goals, mastery goals focus on the learning itself—and tend to be about achieving one's personal best irrespective of how others perform. Students with a mastery goal mindset are more resilient and persistent in their learning, have more positive attitudes toward school, attribute their success to their effort, and use cognitive and metacognitive skills more effectively (Midgley, 2002).

Many of the goals we hold for ourselves are mastery goals. For instance, chances are good that you undertake professional readings in order to strengthen your teaching. You may not be aiming to be Teacher of the Year, but you do want to be a better educator this year than you were last year. The difference between performance and mastery goals is the difference between wanting an *A* in Spanish versus learning to speak Spanish. We aren't suggesting that earning a good grade is an unworthy goal—just that it's crucial to foster a mastery goal orientation to parallel the performance goals already inherent in schooling.

A study of science students ages 13 to 15 suggests doing this will have a lasting positive effect (O'Keefe, Ben-Eliyahu, & Linnenbrink-Garcia, 2013). Students were surveyed during the school year and found to hold predominantly performance-oriented goals. These same students were later enrolled in a three-week summer science enrichment program that was structured to have a "mastery goal–oriented environment." The program was set up to feature curriculum experiences aligned with students' expressed interests. It encouraged intellectual risk taking and investigation (e.g., teachers asked students, "What do you think?" rather than providing answers); provided formative and summative feedback focused on students' learning processes and use of strategies rather than the learning outcomes achieved; and featured a learning environment socially engineered to encourage friendship, peer collaboration, and mutual emotional support. When program participants were surveyed at the end of the summer program, they had shifted from a performance goal orientation toward a mastery goal orientation.

Yes, this is evidence that the structure of the learning environment influences student goals. But the really interesting thing is that when these same students were surveyed a third time, well into the following school year, their mastery goal orientation persisted, even when their current learning environments were performance goal–oriented. The takeaway here is that adopting and strengthening a set of beliefs about mastery can become a part of a learner's internal nature.

So, how can teachers structure the learning environment to enhance a mastery goal orientation? Rather than publicly displaying students' reading performance levels, which encourages competition, social comparison, and a performance goal orientation, perhaps create a bulletin board for students to report on the strategies they are using to improve their reading (e.g., choosing a book with a friend to read and discuss, reading aloud to a younger sibling). When giving students formative feedback, always include mastery goals, such as discussing a student's "personal best" attainments and reviewing his or her growth trajectory on quizzes and tests. You might also survey students about their interests and create learning opportunities that tap into existing mastery goals that are lying just below the surface, waiting to be utilized.

Perhaps the most important way to encourage a mastery goal orientation is to adopt and model it yourself. There is a strong relationship between teachers self-regulating their own learning and the likelihood that a mastery-rich environment exists in their classroom (Gordon, Dembo, & Hocevar, 2007). This is reflective of other research indicating that teachers teach in ways that are consistent with how they themselves learn. Be sure to share with students the experiences you have had with learning something new and why you chose to do so. Dominique paddleboards, and he talks regularly with his students about what he is doing to improve his skills, keeping mastery goals at the center of his conversations. This also gives him opportunities to discuss resilience (see Chapter 3) as a means to persist when facing challenges.

Noah Rodriguez actively works on goal setting with his 7th grade science students, walking them through the process of examining pre-assessment results, developing individual objectives based on the results, and determining evidence of mastery. Here are some evidence-focused goals his students set:

- I will cite my evidence correctly each time I use a source. (Amber)
- I will find evidence that is appropriate for my topic. (Freddy)
- I will collect accurate information and document my process of collection. (Olivia)

As illustrated here, the goals you help your students set should always be developmentally appropriate, and students should have regular opportunities to return to and update their goals as they continue to progress.

Recognizing and Resolving Problems

Another key element of cognitive regulation is a student's ability to recognize and resolve a problem. Finn, the 3rd grade student profiled at the beginning of this chapter, recognized that one problem he needed to face in order to complete his project on time was the week he would be spending at his grandparents' house. His solution was to start the assignment early in order to have a substantial part of it completed before he left. In resolving his problem, Finn drew upon several processes, with support from others.

Solving a problem necessarily begins with recognizing that the problem exists. This is a function of experience and expertise; we learn to anticipate problems in part because we have made mistakes. This is a key premise in the growth mindset research, particularly that one can "fail forward" if given the opportunity to reflect on what contributed to the unsuccessful attempt. It is possible that Finn had previous experience with waiting too long to begin an assignment. We remember writer Anne Lamott's (1995) account of her brother's similar experience, and the subsequent wise advice of their father:

> Thirty years ago my older brother, who was 10 years old at the time, was trying to get a report on birds written that he'd had three months to write. It was due the next day. We were out at our family cabin in Bolinas, and he was at the kitchen table close to tears, surrounded by binder paper and pencils and unopened books on birds, immobilized by the hugeness of the task ahead. Then my father sat down beside him, put his arm around my brother's shoulder, and said, "Bird by bird, buddy. Just take it bird by bird." (p. 19)

Admittedly, making mistakes can be a hard way to learn, but it contributes to problem recognition, especially in seeing a familiar pattern ("Hey, this situation is just like one I faced a few months ago!"). The ability to recognize problems and apply solutions in novel situations is a measure of one's ability to transfer knowledge (Perkins & Salomon, 1992). We see this same ability among elite athletes in team sports and in world-ranked chess players, who seem to be able to anticipate the play evolving on the field or the consequences of a chess move and then play it forward before it has occurred. They rapidly adjust their strategy in order to solve the problem. Once again, it is pattern recognition at work.

Children and adolescents often need support and guidance to recognize and resolve problems. To them, academic or social challenges can seem overwhelming and create paralysis. Of course, this has developmental overtones, too. Very young children benefit from learning the power of an apology as a way to restore a situation. But as children get older, their problems often become more complex.

In the school where we work, teachers follow a problem-solving script to help students develop a plan to tackle challenges they can't seem to resolve on their own:

1. Listen to the student's description of the problem or task.
2. Ask clarifying questions to help the student differentiate the central problem or task from complicating issues or distractions.
3. Restate the problem or task as you understand it, and write it down.
4. Ask the student what the *first* right thing to do would be. Proceed to the next right thing, and the next.
5. Write down the ideas the student offers.
6. If the student is stuck, offer some ideas for how to begin.
7. Make a plan to follow up with the student to see if he or she put the plan into action. (Fisher et al., 2012)

Take the case of Ariel, a 10th grade student having difficulty balancing the workload in her classes. She fell behind in assignments but avoided her teachers rather than seek resolution. After a while, getting back on track seemed impossible to her. But a conversation with her mentor (which involved following the script shown) set Ariel on a course of talking with each teacher and developing a recovery plan to renegotiate two assignments and catch up on the rest.

The same script can be used to help students trying to solve a complex problem in class. (Ariel's math teacher uses it all the time.) It's powerful because it explicitly models how to map out a multistep solution.

Help Seeking

Students with strong cognitive self-regulation are able to distinguish which problems they can solve on their own and which problems (or when within the problem-solving effort) they'll need assistance to solve.

The importance of help seeking and avoidance acumen becomes clear when we consider that children who seek help every time they encounter difficulty or challenge fail to develop the kind of resiliency and grit needed to persevere and become independent learners. Or that children who consistently refuse help (even when it is obvious to their teacher that help is the only pathway to success) can frustrate both themselves and those who teach them.

Well-meaning adults can unwittingly contribute to both of these problems. Take learned helplessness as an example (Maier & Seligman, 1976). The operative word is *learned;* learned helplessness is taught by others and through circumstance. It might be the teacher who provides answers instead of scaffolds, or the teacher who swoops in too quickly and too often to prevent students from struggling.

Let's compare two classroom conversations:

Student: How do you spell *government*?
Teacher: G o v e r n m e n t.

Student: How do you spell *government*?
Teacher: Let's think about this, because I believe you know more than you're giving yourself credit for. What would the root word of *government* be?
Student: Govern.
Teacher: You're right! Can you spell that? Try it on a scrap piece of paper. [Student writes the word *govern*.] Now what's the suffix? Write that down, too, and see if it looks right. [Student adds *-ment*.] What do you think?
Student: I think it's right.
Teacher: You've got it! I use the same strategy when I have to write a word that I'm not sure how to spell. I think about what I might already know about the word, and I write it down to see if it looks right.

Simply telling a student the correct spelling is expeditious, to be sure, and all of us have done exactly this on multiple occasions. Frankly, if the student asking this question were a 1st grader, most of us *would* just furnish the spelling. But if this were an older student, one who already has at least some knowledge that she is not using, the second approach—the problem-solving approach—is a much better choice, empowering the student to leverage her own cognitive resources rather than teaching her that she doesn't need to figure out the spelling herself or that you don't think her capable of figuring it out. Our students aren't helpless, and it's important that we do not teach them to be.

At the other end of the continuum is the student who refuses help when the situation clearly demands it. Think of the toddler rolling around on the floor insisting that he wants to put his own snow boots on even though he lacks the motor skills to do so.

One version of this kind of behavior that you may be familiar with is students who resist taking advantage of the resources provided to help them. We know this scenario well. The school where we work offers numerous tutoring opportunities to assist students with homework, catching up on late assignments, studying for tests, and redoing work that was not successful the first time. We call it *academic recovery*, and we actively promote its use. Yet there are always some students who reject this kind of assistance, even in the face of their failure to complete assignments and demonstrate mastery of content standards.

Woven into their refusal of help are a variety of dispositions and habits, including work avoidance, denial, and automatic reactions to emotionally charged situations. Putting these students on the path to constructive help seeking may require a team effort from teachers who remind them of academic recovery opportunities, administrators who meet individually with them, and family members who pitch in to encourage the development of more productive habits. The work isn't easy, but if we want students to be persistent, we must be, too.

Developing students' ability to decide when they can solve problems independently and when they need (and should accept!) help deserves to be an explicit instructional target. We subscribe to what Sapon-Shevin (1998) calls the *helping curriculum*. She posits that all students need to learn four dimensions of help. We'd actually take that a step further and say not only that students need to learn these four dimensions, but also that mastery of them is essential to a successful personal and professional adult life. Everyone needs to master four problem-solving basics:

1. How to ask for help
2. How to offer help to someone else

3. How to accept help
4. How to politely decline help when you're not ready for it yet

Fourth grade teacher David Greenfield credits the helping curriculum for establishing the kind of emotionally supportive classroom climate his students need to thrive: "I introduced it on the first day of school, and we began with some short lessons in what each of these behaviors looks like and sounds like, and then I use these when it's relevant to talk about decisions characters make in the books and articles we read." His students have noticed that the problem or the resolution in a text is often linked to one of these ideas. For example, the novel *Maniac Magee* (Spinelli, 1990) provided the basis for an ongoing conversation about helping. "We kept a list going throughout the novel of cases where the major characters either correctly or incorrectly enacted one of the helping ideas," Mr. Greenfield said. He noted that helping has become part of the language of the classroom. "When a student is stuck, I hear classmates prompting each other's thinking about help. 'Do you need some help from me, or are you still working it out?' is one I hear a lot," said Mr. Greenfield. "It's pretty awesome to hear them talking with each other in such supportive ways."

Decision Making

The ability to solve problems is directly related to decision making. Nested within resolving a problem is the ability to think about different possibilities or paths, select one, and then take action. The capacity to hold on to two different concepts and think about each is called *cognitive flexibility*. It's expressed in academic tasks such as being able to compare and contrast theories, generating hypotheses, and engaging in consequential thinking to identify cause and effect (Jones et al., 2017).

To develop cognitive flexibility, students need opportunities to make decisions. Young children might vote daily on which of two stories will be read aloud by the teacher. Elementary students might compare and contrast how Christopher Columbus has been portrayed in historical narratives and contemporary writing, and debate the topic. One of our middle school colleagues keeps an active game of Scrabble going as she competes against the class to build words, using it as a means to discuss the strategies they are applying. Secondary students might research the naming of schools honoring Confederate generals and write letters to legislators expressing their opinions.

Building good decision-making skills also requires students to practice reflecting on and evaluating choices made. High school anatomy and physiology teacher Meg Norton uses excerpts from *Guinea Pig Scientists* (Dendy & Boring, 2005) to talk about the decision making of scientists who experimented on themselves. "When we study the infectious disease cycle, we read and discuss the wisdom of Daniel Carrión's decision to inject himself with bartonellosis in order to study it," she said. "Spoiler alert: he died. It's easy in retrospect to say it was a bad decision, but I want them to speculate on how he might have arrived at this choice." As a class, Ms. Norton's students make a list of pros and cons as Carrión would have understood them, as well as a separate list of things he did not know. "Sometimes it is not knowing what we don't know that leads us to bad decisions we make for all the right reasons," Ms. Norton tells them.

Organizational Skills

It's a major turning point in the lives of students when they realize they can't possibly keep all the information they need for school in their heads. They need to write things down and map out processes. They need to study in order to master concepts. In other words, they need to use organizational skills.

Happily, scaffolds to help students develop organizational skills are fairly common—much more so than scaffolds for other components of cognitive self-regulation addressed in this chapter. They include physical and digital organizers such as files and notebooks, which show learners that organizing information and materials makes retrieval much easier; work plans; and teacher-created checklists and time lines to help students plan and revise more complex projects, such as the one Finn completed about the country of Costa Rica.

The ubiquity of organizational scaffolds in the adult world is a reminder that people develop these skills at wildly varying rates and to widely divergent degrees of mastery. Generally speaking, though, middle school seems to be about the time when we see the divide between those who have developed some facility with this aspect of cognitive self-regulation and those who haven't. That divide is particularly wide the area of study skills, which are an important element of organizational skills.

Hattie (2009) groups study skills into three categories:

- *Study tasks,* such as summarizing notes and organizing concepts
- *Metacognition*, especially engaging in self-questioning and monitoring one's learning
- *Dispositions and motivations,* such as setting goals and planning

Collectively, study skills have an effect size of .63, which means they exert a strong influence on learning. Many of these elements have already been discussed in this chapter, but it is important to note that the ability to use each independently is key—in fact, it's a major outcome of cognitive regulation.

One simple approach to building both study skills in particular and organizational skills in general is just to call students' attention to them. Figure 4.1 is adapted from a questionnaire developed by Gordon and colleagues (2007); it's intended to help secondary students gauge their knowledge of organizational and study skills and dispositions. We have reorganized the questions to highlight how the items cluster into categories.

Seventh grade math teacher Juan Carlos Ruiz administers this type of inventory during the first month of school to get his students thinking about their learning processes. "The math they are introduced to this year is pre-algebra, and they have to spend time outside of class to master it," he says. "Lots of kids this age are still stuck on the idea that they just need to memorize algorithms and all will be well. But I need them to think mathematically." The class does several mathematical calculations with the data, including measures of central tendency (i.e., mean, median, mode). Most of all, they discuss the habits of mathematical thinkers. "We have Back-to-School Night in early October, and I have the students prepare a short report on their results, as well as their analysis of their habits," which Mr. Ruiz feels is a good way to get families involved in helping their children.

FIGURE 4.1.
A Learning Process Inventory

Rate each item on a scale of 1–5. Select the answer that best describes your approach to learning.					
Self-Monitoring	Never	Sometimes		Always	
Before a quiz or exam, I plan how I will study the material.	1	2	3	4	5
It is easy for me to establish goals for learning in my classes.	1	2	3	4	5
I have a clear idea of what I am trying to accomplish in my classes.	1	2	3	4	5
When I read a problem, I make sure I know what I am being asked to do before I begin.	1	2	3	4	5
I try to organize an approach in my mind before I actually start problems.	1	2	3	4	5
When I study, I take note of the material I have or have not mastered.	1	2	3	4	5
I organize my study time well.	1	2	3	4	5
When I finish working a problem, I check my answer to see if it is reasonable.	1	2	3	4	5
When I finish working on practice problems, I check my work for errors.	1	2	3	4	5
Deep Strategy	Never	Sometimes		Always	
I work practice problems to check my understanding of new concepts or rules.	1	2	3	4	5
When I work a problem, I analyze it to see if there is more than one way to get the right answer.	1	2	3	4	5
When studying, I try to combine different pieces of information in new ways.	1	2	3	4	5
I draw pictures or diagrams to help me solve problems or piece together new information.	1	2	3	4	5
I work several examples of the same type of problem when studying so that I can understand the problems better.	1	2	3	4	5
I examine example problems that have already been worked to help me figure out how to do similar problems on my own.	1	2	3	4	5
I classify problems into categories before I begin to work them.	1	2	3	4	5

Shallow Processing	Never	Sometimes		Always
I try to memorize the steps for solving problems presented in the text or class.	1	2	3	4	5
When I study for tests, I review my class notes and solved problems.	1	2	3	4	5
When I study, I use solved problems in my notes or the text to help me memorize the steps involved.	1	2	3	4	5
Persistence	Never	Sometimes		Always
If I have trouble understanding a problem, I go over it again until I understand it.	1	2	3	4	5
When I run into a difficult homework problem, I give up and go on to the next problem.	1	2	3	4	5
Environmental Structuring	Never	Sometimes		Always
I arrange a place to study without distractions.	1	2	3	4	5
I isolate myself from anything that distracts me.	1	2	3	4	5
I do all my studying in a place where I can concentrate.	1	2	3	4	5

Source: Adapted with permission from "Do Teachers' Own Learning Behaviors Influence Their Classroom Goal Orientation and Control Ideology?" by S. C. Gordon, M. H. Dembo, and D. Hocevar, 2007. This article was published in *Teaching & Teacher Education, 23.* Copyright Elsevier, 2007.

"Middle school math gets more challenging, and parents aren't always sure how they can help. So I show them. Talking about good organizational skills and mastery goals is the best way they can help."

Takeaways

Teaching students cognitive regulation is an important aspect of social and emotional learning. When you provide students with appropriate learning opportunities, you create a classroom environment that is more focused and intentional. The objective is to ensure students understand that they have the power to recognize their own thinking, pay attention (and develop skills to regain their focus if needed), set and monitor their goals, recognize and resolve problems, develop decision-making skills, and become increasingly organized.

QUESTIONS FOR REFLECTION

1. Do you model metacognitive thinking for students? Do you provide students opportunities to practice and develop their own metacognitive skills?

2. What tools do you have to focus students' attention? Do you provide students feedback about their ability to refocus on learning when their attention wanders?

3. Do you set goals with your students? If so, what types of goal are they? Do students have the opportunity to revisit the goals they set to monitor progress?

4. Have you explicitly taught students to recognize and resolve problems? Do you provide them sufficient time to do so?

5. Have you explicitly taught students how to make decisions? Do you allow them opportunities to make decisions and learn from their decisions when there were better choices?

6. What organizational skills do your students need to develop? How can you address those needs within the flow of classroom learning?

CHAPTER 5

Social Skills

Prosocial skills | Sharing | Teamwork
Relationship building | Communication
Empathy | Relationship repair

Eighth grader Anissa enters her history classroom late. She hands her tardy slip to her teacher without saying anything. Anissa is usually talkative and friendly, and Mr. Garcia notices the change in demeanor.

Within a few moments, Anissa has joined her learning station group, one of four set up to provide active investigation of immigration from Northern Europe to the United States between 1800 and 1860. She is supposed to start in on her independent learning task, but instead, she just sits.

Mr. Garcia walks over to Anissa's desk and asks her if she wants to talk. When she looks up, her eyes are welling with tears. "Let's go sit at my desk for a few minutes," Mr. Garcia says quietly, gesturing to the "talking chair" next to his desk. All his students know that if they sit in this particular over-sized chair, they can share whatever is on their minds. Sometimes they come to sit in this chair between periods, during lunch, or after school. They have learned that Mr. Garcia does not pry but will offer a sympathetic ear.

"It's no big deal, really," Anissa says, once she's settled. "It's just that a friend posted some mean things on Snap last night, and I told her it was not right. It's about someone else, but if someone did that to me, I would be mad. And I would be worried about what other people thought."

"It's really hard when people you care about do things that you don't agree with," Mr. Garcia responds. "It makes you question the relationship. What did she say when you told her it wasn't right?"

"She got mad at me and said that I was a traitor."

"That's really hard," Mr. Garcia says. "When you do the right thing and there are negative consequences, it can make you not want to do the right thing the next time. Like we've talked about before, it's not easy to keep doing the right thing when it's not the popular thing. Can I ask something else? Is the other person safe? Was the posting bad enough that we need to talk with Dr. Castillo [the principal]?"

Anissa shakes her head. "No, it was just rude. And she took it down anyway. I just don't know how to keep my friend and do the right thing at the same time. Can we talk more after school?"

"Of course," Mr. Garcia says. "You can always talk with me. I think this might be lesson in empathy for others, and it's allowing you to understand somebody else's perspective. There are ways to repair relationships when both parties want to. I look forward to our conversation."

The kind of struggle Anissa was having with her friend are not an uncommon occurrence in the lives of young people. Social media make navigating these waters terribly complex, as slights and hurt feelings are amplified in ways we adults never experienced when we were school aged. As students work through these choppy waters, our counsel is more important than ever. Of course, inserting yourself into an adolescent's personal troubles is always tricky, and it is just as likely that Anissa never would have opened up to Mr. Garcia in the first place. But a few things worked in his favor (and hers):

- Mr. Garcia noticed that Anissa wasn't her usual self. You have to know students in order to be able to see that something isn't right.
- He and Anissa had forged a relationship that allowed for an impromptu conversation to take place.
- Mr. Garcia was able to leverage SEL themes of empathy and relationship repair that he had previously discussed in his class. Once the

groundwork for discussing social skills has been laid, the work of helping students develop them gets easier.

• Positive social skills and positive relationships, essential in the classroom and in life, are contagious, and so are negative ones (Marsden,
1998). Poor relationships quickly spread to others and undermine
learning. This is why there must be an investment in teaching social
skills and positive relationships at the individual and classroom levels.
A study of nearly 1,800 adolescents found that the well-being of the
individual student predicted the well-being of his or her classmates,
and vice versa (King & Datu, 2017). Mr. Garcia's attention to Anissa's
well-being bodes well for the relationships of the students in the classroom. And here is a vital concept that should not be overlooked: relationships begin with *you*. You are a broker in developing relationships
between and among students.

Social Skills Defined

Human beings are hardwired to socialize—to affiliate with one another to
achieve group goals. In fact, it was when our species gained the ability to
cooperate and collaborate that human development skyrocketed (Pinker,
2012). Language, tools, and processes could be shared across generations
and societies. Humans have developed prosocial skills that are found within
all cultures. Most of the dispositions discussed in previous chapters are primarily internal to the individual but play a role in the expression of prosocial
skills, which involve interactions with others.

Prosocial skills include helping behaviors (see Chapter 4) as well as
sharing and teamwork, which are examined in more detail in this chapter.
These prosocial skills are proactive (hence the name), meaning that they
are foundational to, but not the same as, developing relationships with others. In other words, you can have good prosocial skills but not have strong
relationships. Consider the number of times each day that you engage in the
prosocial skills of helping, sharing, and teamwork behaviors with people with
whom you have no relationship. Holding the door for someone, moving over
on a subway seat so another passenger can sit down, and standing patiently in

line at the supermarket are all prosocial skills that help us function as a group, even when we are strangers. Prosocial skills contribute to social competence.

Prosocial skills are prerequisite to, but not the same as, building and maintaining relationships, some of which blossom into friendships. Relationships require another set of skills—communication, empathy, and methods for repairing relationships when they are damaged. Empathy, which is the ability to understand and share the experiences and feelings of others, is a critical driver in relationships. A well-developed sense of empathy is necessary for altruistic decision making, where the good of others is taken into account. Relationship skills are more complex and require lots of adult guidance and brokering to help children and adolescents become more competent. We will begin with an examination of the prosocial skills of sharing and teamwork that transform classrooms into communities.

Prosocial Skills

Prosocial behaviors are influenced by the expectations of others. They are sometimes referred to as *normative* behaviors, meaning they reflect societal norms—agreements about the right or most the desirable way to behave (e.g., older children should grant more latitude to younger children).

Collective opinion carries weight, which is why it is so useful to create classroom norms that go beyond standard compliance measures (e.g., raise your hand before speaking, keep your feet flat on the floor). There is evidence that children and adults engage in more frequent prosocial behaviors when there is an audience and when the influence of the social norms of the setting are strong (House & Tomasello, 2018). The school where the three of us work operates on three norms that are prosocial in nature:

1. Take care of yourself.
2. Take care of each other.
3. Take care of this place.

Of course, operationalizing these norms requires significant investment in the principles of social and emotional learning profiled in this book. Beginning with the first week of school, students and teachers list ways in which these principles are demonstrated in the classroom. From there, teachers and students co-construct classroom rules that align with these prosocial norms. Science classrooms usually have specific rules about lab equipment ("Take care of this place"), but many rules circle around the second norm ("Take care of each other"). Examples include "Listen respectfully even when you don't agree" and "Yield the floor so others can speak." In these rules lie the mechanisms of teamwork.

Prosocial behaviors cluster into three categories: *sharing*, *helping*, and *teamwork*. Because we discussed helping in Chapter 4's discussion of cognitive regulation, we won't return to it again. But we will dig into sharing, which is a precursor to altruism, and teamwork, which includes cooperation in the classroom.

Sharing

Anyone who has been around very young children can confirm that early sharing behavior is often . . . reluctant. Often, it's a response to the prompting of adults or older siblings, accompanied by a reminder that sharing is the right or fair thing to do—thus identifying it as a societal norm. Primary and early-elementary teachers can (and often do) follow this same model, adding normative information to classroom rules to help establish expectations beyond the rule "Share." Compare: "It's time to share the ball with someone else now" and "It's time to share the ball now with someone else who's been waiting. That's one way we take care of each other."

Willingly sharing resources and materials can be a challenge for some children, but as a foundational skill for positive relationships, it's worth promoting and practicing. Consider that primary-aged children perceive partial resource sharing as a sign of friendship between the two (Liberman & Shaw, 2017). Kindergarten teacher Kiley Farmer plays turn-taking games with her students to build habits about the give-and-take nature of cooperation and sharing. "I start the year by reading *It's Mine!* (Lionni, 1996), which is about three frogs that squabble with each other until a storm comes along and they realize how much they need each other," she said. We hang a picture of the frogs to remind us not to be too 'froggy' with each other." Ms. Farmer makes sure to set up her learning environment so that her students get lots of practice sharing. "Art supplies, math manipulatives, tablets . . . I often stage it so that two students will need to work together with one set of materials. As they get better at sharing, I expand the group sizes to three or four. It's a good way to build their teamwork skills," she said.

Teamwork

The ability to productively collaborate with others is widely understood as an essential skill. This prosocial behavior is variously described as a 21st-century skill (Partnership for 21st Century Learning, 2015) or, in the world of work, a "soft skill" (SCANS, 1992). The ability to collaborate with others draws on a number of other social and emotional skills, including positive relationships, communication, self-regulation, goal setting, and taking responsibility. Teamwork is required in many childhood endeavors (e.g., sports, music, theater, play). In school, the importance of teamwork is usually expressed through a variety of group tasks that require mutual participation to complete the task. We define *collaborative learning* as a set of practices designed to foster peer-to-peer interactions through meaningful academic tasks (Fisher & Frey, 2014).

Simply pushing four desks together is no guarantee that collaboration will happen. Too often we have seen students divide and conquer a task, working together only for a short period of time to stitch together the parts they have developed separately. Eighth grade humanities teacher Clay Westerbrook had noticed this happening for several years when his students did group presentations. "The kids would get up there and each person would talk about the one presentation slide they produced. No one could ever answer a question about a partner's slide. Sometimes, they wouldn't even match visually," he said. However, he didn't really know what to do about it. Things changed for him when he looked at the experience through the lens of task complexity: "I was giving them an assignment where they didn't really need each other. All they were doing was cutting and pasting information from the internet."

Mr. Westbrook made two important changes. The first change was to use peer evaluations. His students completed feedback forms about the content and the presentation style to share publicly with the group presenting. "This really improved their ability to remain engaged and to practice ways to give feedback that are useful." But the second change to the process—introducing iterative presentations—really fostered teamwork: He introduced iterative presentations. Instead of being assigned a topic, Mr. Westbrook's teams had to identify content based on a previous team's presentation. The teacher gives the first presentation, then draws the name of a team to create a second one. Based on the initial presentation, the team must identify the topic for their 5-minute presentation. "I give them the rest of the class period to put it together, so they have to stay in close communication with one another," he said. While that team is building the presentation, Mr. Westbrook works with the rest of the class. The team delivers their short presentation at the beginning of the next class, then draws the name of a second team. The second team's task is to put together a presentation that answers a question derived from the previous topic. "I call it Presentation Shark Tank," he said. For example, to get the ball rolling during the Creating America unit of study, "I started with a short presentation on manifest destiny. The first team wondered about the Oregon Trail, which I had mentioned, so they presented on that topic the following day." Over the next week, teams presented on the perils faced by mountain men and settlers, the Donner Party, displaced western Native American tribes, the Louisiana Purchase, the lives of Seminoles in the Everglades, and the fight for the Alamo. "It really prompts a new kind of listening, too, because a team doesn't know whether they will be selected until the end of the presentation."

Tracking the development of teamwork skills is possible using the Teamwork Scale for Youth (Lower, Newman, & Anderson-Butcher, 2017). This eight-item self-report instrument has been validated for use with students ages 9–15 and can be used multiple times in a school year to monitor progress. The students respond to the following statements using a Likert scale of 1 (*not at all true*) to 5 (*really true*):

- I feel confident in my ability to work in a team.
- I know how to give my team members feedback that will not hurt their feelings.
- I ask others for feedback.
- I make an effort to include other members of my group.
- I value the contributions of my team members.
- I treat my team members as equal members of the team.
- I am good at communicating with my team members.
- I feel confident in my ability to be a leader. (p. 719)

As with other assessment tools of this type, students' answers can open the door for having future conversations, setting goals, and celebrating growth.

Relationship Building

Relationships are critical in the learning lives of students. The relationship between teacher and student exerts a strong influence on achievement, reported by Hattie (2009) as having an effect size of .52. As well, when we strive to build relationships with students, we model how it is that they can do so with others, including peers. Therefore, before discussing ways to foster peer relationships, it is crucial that we attend to how we ourselves model by example the kinds of healthy relationships we want in our classrooms.

Student-Teacher Relationships

All relationships, regardless of the age of the people involved, are predicated on a foundation of respect and regard. We can't demand that students form healthy relationships with peers if we don't ourselves demonstrate the value of respect and regard we hold for our own students. Students look to us for guidance in how in-school relationships should be formed. To lay the foundation for healthy, growth-producing relationships with students, educators need to do the following:

- Know students' names and know how to pronounce those names correctly.

- Be mindful of the attitude we communicate through verbal and non-verbal language, including facial expressions, and how this can make students feel welcomed (or not).
- Know students' interests and find things for them to learn and read that honor and help them explore and expand those interests.
- Make positive connections with students' families through home visits, phone calls, or e-mail.
- Provide quality instruction that is relevant for students.

There is an adage in education that students don't care how much you *know* until they know how much you *care*. Caring is an important part of a relationship. When we use people's names correctly, speak to them about their interests, and seek to make connections to their lives, we are drawing a blueprint for how relationships are built. We exhibit caring behaviors so that in turn students can use them with each other.

Effective student-teacher relationships are trusting and supportive, but they are also characterized by high expectations. In other words, "caring" is not just about "being nice." Students expect to be challenged *and* supported; what they need are teachers who are "warm demanders" (Vasquez, 1989). Delpit (2012) notes that warm demanders "expect a great deal of their students, convince them of their own brilliance, and help them to reach their potential in a disciplined and structured environment" (p. 77). That's the type of relationship that accelerates learning.

When it comes to practical things you can do to position yourself to be a warm demander, we direct you to the work of Mark Finnis (2018) of Independent Thinking (www.independentthinking.co.uk), who has developed a list of 33 ways to build better relationships with students (see Figure 5.1).

Peer Relationships

When students experience healthy, growth-producing relationships with their teachers, they are more likely to mirror those actions and behaviors with their peers. By teaching students to engage with peers and develop respect for one another, we provide them with avenues for dealing more productively with problems. Students with healthy relationships tend to work

FIGURE 5.1

33 Ways to Build Better Relationships with Students

1.   Be who you needed when you were at school.
2.   Connect before content.
3.   Make regular deposits into the "social capital" bank.
4.   Small ripples create big waves; do the simple things well.
5.   Don't worry about doing things 100 percent better; rather, do 100 things 1 percent better.
6.   Know your children well and allow them to know you well.
7.   Don't be afraid of the "L word" . . . Love. Spread it thick.
8.   Some children come to school to learn, others to be loved.
9.   Every child (and adult) needs a champion.
10. Engagement has three forms: physical, emotional, and mental.
11. The language we use creates the reality we experience.
12. "Difficult child" or "child with difficulties"? "Troubled family" or a "family with troubles"?
13. Get involved earlier in the life of the child, earlier in the life of the problem.
14. Separate the deed from the doer.
15. Healthy relationships are built on high challenge and high support.
16. Punishment creates resentment rather than reflection.
17. There are always three truths: my truth, your truth, and the truth.
18. The best apology is changed behavior.
19. The "small stuff" is the big stuff.
20. Create a sense of belonging.
21. Catch them getting it right more than you catch them getting it wrong.
22. Magnify strengths rather than weaknesses, and focus on gifts rather than deficits.
23. The language we use to describe an experience often becomes the experience.
24. Difficult conversations—do they have to be? Remember, there is no easy way to poke people in the eye. However we do it, it's going to sting a little.
25. Strike when the iron's cold.
26. We learn to care by being cared for.
27. If you're not modeling what you're teaching, you're teaching something different.
28. Listening is what you do to understand, not time spent simply waiting to reply.
29. Silence isn't a gap in the conversation; it is part of the conversation.
30. Culture exists in every organization, but is yours by design or by default?
31. Everything looks better when you put it in a circle.
32. Smile at children; it's good for you both.
33. There is always another way.

Source: Adapted with permission from "33 Ways to Build Better Relationships," by M. Finnis. Copyright 2018 by Independent Thinking.

through issues rather than express their anger on a social media platform or with their fists. Although peer relationships require more than modeling from adults, the examples adults provide students set the expectations for their interactions with others.

Feeling a sense of belonging to a group is essential for our well-being as social animals. Adolescence is a particularly challenging time, and teenagers are especially vulnerable to feeling alienated and marginalized. At this developmental stage, relationships with peers grow in importance, and feeling disliked is associated with loss of learning, with a −.19 effect size (Hattie, 2009), equivalent to roughly a half a year of lost learning. A measure of relationships is the extent to which one feels a sense of relatedness to others—in other words, connected to others. *Relatedness* is defined as one's perception that peers care about you, respect you, and see you as a valued member of a group or team. A study of nearly 1,100 middle and high school students in 65 schools found that peer relatedness was stronger in classrooms where helping behaviors were valued, and where students had opportunities to interact academically with one another (Mikami, Ruzeck, Hafen, Gregory, & Allen, 2017). Although teachers are not able to make friendships materialize out of thin air, we can set the stage for relationships to strengthen among our students.

Ninth grade history teacher Aja Buchanan structures her classroom so that students get to know one another from the first day. They introduce themselves by writing a short biography, then convert the text into a word cloud graphic of their own design. "They love seeing their work displayed," she smiled. "Never too old for that." She makes a point of making sure that she and everyone else in the room learns each other's names by the end of the first week, reinforcing that a sign of respect is using one another's names correctly. She designs her instruction to emphasize collaborative learning ("I tell them my goal is that about half of the instructional minutes during the week are going to be in small groups, so they should get used to it"), then proceeds to teach the communication skills needed to function well as a member of a team. "These are life skills, not just history skills. I tell them, 'If you're able to establish a relationship with other people quickly, it makes work and life just a little bit easier,'" said Ms. Buchanan.

Another reason relationships with others are important is they help us develop our identity and agency. Mike Holmes's 5th grade class hosts a short "gratitude circle" once a week, during which students share their appreciation for each other. "This brief activity provides students a healthy transition back to the learning environment and some practice with oral language skills, not to mention relationship building," he said. At the start of the year, it's often hard for students to accept the compliments, Mr. Holmes told us. "They get better at it, though," he added. "I love to watch their confidence and pride in themselves grow."

On one particular afternoon, the students shared the following compliments:

- "Andrew, thank you for helping me today with my math problems. You didn't tell me the answers, but you helped me a lot."
- "Dulce, it made me happy when you invited me to play at lunch. I probably would have just sat at the table."
- "Najeed, you sing really good. Someday, you should sing for our class."
- "Taylor, you are so brave. I don't think you are afraid of anything."

Relationship with the School

Finally, students who do not have a good relationship with their school and believe they are valued members of the school community will be likely to exhibit the desire to repair harm when it occurs.

Our goal is for students to develop the habit of thinking before they act, reflecting on the actions they do take, and learning from the experience. Relationships students have with adults in the school can be highly influential in this process. Students who respect these adults don't often engage in problematic behavior. When they do, they have to face the adults they care about and make amends for what they have done. We also hope that our students reach the point when they care about the school as a whole, and decide not to take certain actions because they don't want the school to be affected in a negative way. This is a long-term goal that requires a significant amount of investment, but when students reach that pinnacle in their thinking, great changes occur.

At the school where we work, students' relationships with the school are at the center of what we do. We describe the process in more detail in *How to Create a Culture of Achievement in Your School and Classroom* (Fisher et al., 2012), using five pillars intended to build affiliation between the organization and the students who learn there. Briefly:

- *Welcome* is our investment in policies for how students and their families feel a sense of belonging.
- *Do No Harm* is our investment in restorative practices.
- *Choice Words* is our investment in using language that supports students' sense of identity and agency.
- *Never Too Late to Learn* is our investment in policies related to academic and behavioral interventions.
- *Best School in the Universe* is our investment in ourselves as we engage in continuous improvement.

We are reminded of Miguel, an 11th grader who was identified as credit deficient. He had been expelled at the end of the 9th grade and never attended 10th grade. He showed up at a school on the first day of what would have been his junior year only because his probation officer wanted evidence of his enrollment. He was defiant and disengaged (but at least he was in school). Miguel made several mistakes and had poor attendance. Yet there was an English teacher who made a connection with him. She would advocate for him every time something went wrong. She started brokering relationships between him and other teachers, and Miguel's behavior started to change. At one point he said his behavior changed because "these people here are trying and they really care. When I do something wrong it makes them all look bad. I don't want it to reflect on this school, so I keep my *$%# together now." Yes, one bad word but Miguel graduated and is working as a mechanic. That wouldn't have happened without a trusting relationship and the eventual development of respect for the school.

Communication

Relationships with peers, teachers, and the school are built, deepened, and repaired through effective communication. Communication is also an essential vehicle for learning. Students are expected to read, write, speak, and listen as part of their learning. And there are specific communication standards (often called *language arts*) that focus teachers' efforts to develop this aspect of learning. Yet many people, old and young alike, have difficulty communicating, especially when it comes to expressing ideas, feelings, and reactions to emotionally charged situations. It may be because some classrooms limit communication to specific, safe topics. Or it may be because we don't test speaking and listening, which means these skills receive less attention in the classroom. Or it may be because teachers assume students know how to communicate and thus do not focus on these skills.

As noted in Chapter 3, the willingness to listen is a marker of emotional regulation. It is also a skill needed in effective communication, as well as for relationship building. Unfortunately, for a lot of students, the opposite of speaking is waiting to speak again, rather than listening. There are a number of models for active listening, but the common aspects of these models can be summed up like this:

- *Be attentive.* Focus on the person talking and let the person finish talking. Track the person speaking, even if you don't make eye contact with the person. Keep your mind on the topic and try not to let it wander to other topics. You might do this by trying to visualize what the person is saying.
- *Ask related or probing questions.* Keep your questions focused on the topic or a related topic. Don't use questions to steer the conversation away from the topic but rather allow the person to clarify ideas or provide examples.
- *Request clarification.* If something is not clear, ask for additional information. Don't assume you know what the person means; invite the person to explain it.
- *Paraphrase.* Recap the key points by rephrasing them in your own words. This allows you to check for your own understanding and to show the person you are listening.
- *Notice emotions and feelings.* Recognize the message as well as the emotions that are sent with the content of the message.
- *Summarize.* Don't just end the conversation suddenly. Instead, summarize what you talked about, any agreements reached, or any areas that still need discussion.

The students in Alexis Calvio's 4th grade class have developed their listening skills because their teacher regularly asks them what they heard another student say and if they agree or disagree with that person. For example, while discussing the characteristics of inventors after reading several articles about different inventors, she asked her students to discuss their ideas with their team. Ms. Calvio used Numbered Heads Together to encourage students to support each other. Here's what it looked like.

Students sat at numbered tables in the classroom and counted off, 1 through 5, so that every person had a number. Following their initial conversation, Ms. Calvio rolled a die and told the class that Person 4 from each table should be ready to answer. The students talked again, this time making sure that Person 4 at their table was prepared to answer. Ms. Calvio brought the class back together, rolled the die again, and called out, "Table 6!"

Kanella from Table 6 stood up and spoke confidently: "One of the characteristics that inventors need to have is creativity, because you have to be able to think of new ideas that the world needs. If you invent something that no one needs, then you won't be able to sell it."

Ms. Calvio rolled the die again, and it was Table 1's turn. In this technique, Round 2 of the discussion requires students to agree or disagree with the previous round's speaker and offer a reason why. Maya stood up and said, "I agree with Kanella that inventors need to be creative, but I don't think it is just because they need to sell the invention. Even if some of the new things won't sell, they're still an inventor."

There is evidence that students learn through collaborative conversations like these (Frey, Fisher, & Nelson, 2013). For too many students, learning is stifled because they have not yet developed the skills required to interact productively with their peers. Relationships are important, but so are all of the other aspects of SEL that we discuss in this book. Communication cannot be limited to academic conversations; students need to talk through social situations as well.

Another way that teachers can build listening and communications skills is through the use of circles. Communication circles allow students to learn about their own perspectives and those of others. Circles are part of "restorative practices" work (e.g., Smith, Fisher, & Frey, 2015) and can serve as a foundation for repairing harm when it is done. Without experience communicating one's feelings in the low-stakes environment of communication circles, for example, a student may not be willing to engage in higher-stakes conferences when damage or harm has been done.

Communication circles show students that their experiences are valid, that they are allowed to share their feelings, and that peers listen to their thinking. Regardless of the type of circle, there are responsibilities and expectations:

- Each student should have the chance to share or be encouraged to share.
- Students should talk to each other, not the facilitator.
- Circles should not be used solely for discipline.

Our experiences suggest that the topics need to be safe when introducing circle processes. These low-stakes circles use questions for which there is no "right" answer, making them less emotionally charged. Here are some examples:

- If you had a superpower, what would it be, and why?
- If you could be an animal, which would you choose? Why?
- What is your dream vacation?
- What is one word that best describes you?
- If you were stuck on an island, what one thing would you want?
- What is your favorite color?

When students understand the process and know that the experience is psychologically safe, circles can be used to discuss more complex issues such as classroom operations, bullying on the playground, fears about an upcoming test, or struggles with relationships. The opening question is really important. A teacher who begins with the question, "What can I do to make this class run more smoothly?" sets the stage for a discussion or a critique centered around the teacher. Contrast this with the opening question, "What can *we* do to make this classroom run more smoothly?" This phrasing indicates shared responsibility for the construction of the learning environment. The focus of the circle, regardless of the topic, is everyone's growth and reflection.

Sequential Communication Circles

Sequential circles allow each member of the group an opportunity to partic-ipate in the conversation. We recommend forming the circle out of chairs alone (not desks) or even having the students stand or sit on the floor. The goal is communication; you want everyone to make eye contact. Typically there is an object, such as a stuffed animal or tennis ball, that students pass around the circle. Only the person with the object can talk. Sequential cir-cles are suitable for situations when you want full participation by members. However, we don't want to force students to speak when they don't want to. Those who are not ready to speak can pass.

Sixth grade teacher Dahlia Colangelo was preparing her students for an annual tradition—the districtwide five-day camping experience for 6th grad-ers held in the mountains a few miles outside the city. Ms. Colangelo does this prep every year. For most students in her urban district, it's their first camping experience, and for many, it's the first night they'll spend away from home in an unfamiliar place. Her students are always excited about the trip, but there is also anxiety and insecurity just below the surface.

Because Ms. Colangelo understands that modeling can be an effective way for showing others how to communicate and how to express their feel-ings (e.g., Miller, 1989), she began by saying this:

> We've covered a lot of information about our camping trip next week, and I'm excited. But I'm also a little bit nervous. I get butterflies before these trips. I wonder if you do, too. Let's go around the circle and start by naming one thing we're excited about. I'll start. I'm excited about the hike we'll do on Tuesday morning. I can't wait for you to see my favorite spot on the trail. I want to share it with you.

Ms. Colangelo passed the "talking stick" (a small souvenir vinyl football from the local university team) to Ariyana, the student to her left. "What are you excited about?" the teacher asked. In short order, the talking stick was passed around the circle, and each student named an event he or she was looking forward to. When it was Ms. Colangelo's turn again, she moved the conversation forward:

I get nervous, too, when I'm getting ready for this trip. Sometimes it's something I'm worried about. I'm worried that because I won't see my own kids for the whole week, that something might go wrong without me there. Ariyana, what is something about the trip that you are nervous or worried about?

The pace was a little slower as students revealed their trepidations. Being away from home was a big one. Then several students in a row talked about insects and snakes before the talking stick reached Eliana, who voiced this fear: "I'm nervous about sharing a cabin with three other people. Like changing clothes. Will people make fun of me?" This worry was echoed by some other students. When it was Ms. Colangelo's turn again, she complimented them on their courage, then said, "I heard some people saying that a worry they have is about privacy. What are some ways we can help each other feel a little less worried about this?" This third round elicited ideas, and when it was Ms. Colangelo's turn once again, she summarized their thoughts and invited discussion about agreements. The class even adopted a slogan ("What happens at camp stays at camp") as a reminder that unexpected things would happen. Some might be funny or embarrassing, but they agreed that they would not tease one another. Ms. Colangelo said, "It might not help us with mosquito bites, but it's good to know that we're all going to protect each other this way."

Non-Sequential Communication Circles

Non-sequential circles operate much the same as sequential circles, except that students do not speak in order of their position. In a non-sequential circle, the current speaker recognizes the next person to speak. The facilitator rarely interrupts the flow of the conversation unless it is necessary to get the discussion back on track.

One morning, during Rebecca Phillip's 10th grade English class, Angel raised his hand and asked if they could have a circle. The class was engaged in a unit that included reading the short story "All the Years of Her Life" (Callaghan, 1936), which focuses on a mother's devotion to her son, forgiveness, moral choices, and the consequences of one's actions.

Once seated in a circle, Angel confessed that he was having a hard time paying attention to the text because it was hitting really close to home: "It reminded me of when my mother said to me, 'You have shamed me enough.' It was because of my grades and how I'm acting at home. I'm not sure how to fix that relationship."

The students responded with advice, compassion, and empathy. Some wanted to know more about Angel's situation at home. Others offered to help him catch up on grades before the next reporting period. Still others shared experiences about conflict with their families and how they resolved it. For example, Liam had this advice for Angel:

Own it. And then do something about it. Your attitude is your choice. Go home tonight and tell her you're sorry. And then show her respect. She's your momma . . . the only one you got. Yeah, she'll get on your nerves, but practice what we learned. Take a breath. Think before you speak. Talk it through. It's worth it. You don't know what I would do to have one more convo with my moms.

Angel ended the circle by saying, "Can we have this circle again next week? This was good for me. I think I can get back to the reading now."

Ms. Phillip later reflected that emotional work is part of teaching literature. "The characters we read about help my students think about the world writ large. So sometimes we need to allow for some group processing." She told us her students' writing is now stronger "because they understand that literature is a reflection of the world and can shape how we think about the world and our place in it."

Fishbowl Communication Circles

The fishbowl strategy takes place in a circle within a circle. Those in the outer circle witness and listen to the discussion held by those in the inner circle. There is an empty chair or two in the inner circle to allow people from the outer circle to participate temporarily in the inner circle.

The students in Charles Lee's 2nd grade class needed a fishbowl circle discussion following some hurt feelings on the playground during recess. Mr.

Lee started the circle by saying, "I heard that we didn't live up to one of our goals today. Does anyone remember the goals we set? Who would like to join the inner circle to talk about it?" Several children moved to the inner circle.

Jamal volunteered, saying, "We made a goal that we would take care of each other. But today, we had problems at recess."

Kevin added, "We stopped taking care of each other because we all wanted to play kickball and there wasn't enough spaces."

Diego responded, "We told them that they couldn't play and then they took the ball away so we couldn't play."

"We should've taken turns with a timer," Ruben said. "But nobody got to play because we didn't take care of each other."

Jamal left the inner circle and was replaced by Carly, who said, "Oh, it was about kickball? I thought it was because I didn't take care of Aimee on the jungle gym when she needed me to. I'm sorry, Aimee. I just got mad and didn't do my strategy."

The conversation continued with students taking responsibility for their actions at recess and making commitments to one another to work harder to reach their goal.

Some people worry about the amount of time spent in circles and the potential loss of learning time. In this case, if students were still focused on their conflicts from recess and didn't have a chance to process and deal with them, they likely would have had difficulty attending to Mr. Lee's planned math lesson. The few minutes they spent in the circle accomplished several things. First, it allowed students to recognize and express their feelings. Second, it provided a way to move on from the problems at recess. Third, it allowed them to practice communication skills, including listening and turn taking (which are included in the grade-level standards). Finally, it gave the class the ability to focus on the math lesson once the conflict had been addressed.

Empathy

Empathy, being able to understand the feelings of others, is an important component of relationship development. Although there is limited evidence that empathy can be directly taught, it can be developed by giving students opportunities to engage in empathetic responses. Some guidelines for fostering empathy advise educators to be aware of their own actions, integrate literature that allows students to explore empathy for historical and contemporary characters, and mirror empathetic responses to their students (e.g., Gerdes, Segal, Jackson, & Mullins, 2011; Gordon, 2009).

There are also specific actions that teachers can take that are likely to result in students' empathy development. Here are some to try:

- *Label the feeling.* As we noted in Chapter 3, students need to understand their emotional responses to various situations. An extension of that skill is being able to accurately identify the emotions of others. For example, a teacher might say, "I noticed that you went over to talk with Paul when he was sitting by himself. He might have felt lonely, or he might have wanted some time to think."

- *Encourage students to talk about their feelings.* Also noted in Chapter 3, talking about feelings is an important part of SEL. For students to develop empathy, they need to learn to talk about the feelings of others, not just their own—and this includes the feelings of teachers and the characters students encounter in literature. Teachers can use the tools outlined in Chapter 3 to encourage students to talk about the feelings of others. This is easier for students to do when they are able to understand and label their own feelings. For instance, a teacher might say, "Listen to the dialogue in this scene once again. How would you describe how this character is feeling right now? What would you say to him?"

- *Praise empathetic behavior.* When students demonstrate empathy, it should be noted and appreciated. A challenge with empathy is that it's not always about positive feelings. When someone is hurt or sad, being empathetic means the student understands what it means to feel hurt and sad. A teacher might say, "You noticed that the game wasn't fair. You know what it feels like when something is not fair, and you talked with other students to make it more fair. I appreciate your efforts and I hope you are feeling proud of yourself."

- *Teach nonverbal cues.* With care, students can learn to notice nonverbal cues that indicate the emotional status of others. We say "with care" because it would be insensitive to stop a class and prompt everyone look at an angry or happy student and then talk about how that student is communicating emotion without words. It's easier to do this with videos and picture books, pausing at moments to identify the nonverbal cues for students. A teacher might say, "I'm really moved by the expression on this character's face in this picture. When you see someone with that expression, what do you do and say?"

- *Don't use anger to control students.* When teachers (and parents) use anger to control children, the children may comply—but it often comes at the cost of learning. When an adult says, "I'm very angry with you," or demonstrates anger nonverbally, students shut down and withdraw. Teachers can express disappointment and reset expectations, but when anger enters the interaction, learning is compromised. For example, rather than say, "I'm angry with you and you owe me five minutes of lunch," a teacher might say, "When you left the room without telling me, I was worried about your safety and that I was not doing my job. Can you tell me what was going on? What commitments can you make and what consequences seem reasonable?"

- *Give students jobs that require empathy.* Taking care of living things promotes empathy. Watering the plants in the classroom, monitoring the butterfly garden, or taking care of a classroom pet are just some ways to give students experience with empathetic responses. There is some evidence that students learn altruism and caring as they learn responsibility (e.g., Mattis et al., 2009). Being responsible for distributing and collecting materials also can help students develop an ethic of care and altruistic thinking. A teacher might ask a student, "Can you make sure that Madeline the rabbit has enough water? It's our responsibility to make sure she has what she needs."

There is evidence that empathy develops as students explore literature and discuss the actions of characters. For example, the students in Jose Herrera's 5th grade class were reading *The One and Only Ivan* (Applegate,

2015), the story of a gorilla who lives in a cage in a shopping mall. Told from Ivan the gorilla's point of view, readers learn that he seems satisfied until he reevaluates his life from the perspective of a baby elephant taken from her family. The students in Mr. Herrera's class discussed the story, acknowledging not only the anthropomorphism but also the feelings that the author assigned to the gorilla. One of the students said, "It's not just about Ivan. This is how people would feel if they lost a family member." Another student noted, "You can't always fix things, but you can be a friend."

We'd like to share an additional strategy drawn from restorative practices that can foster empathy with students and equip them with another communication technique. *Affective statements* allow teachers (and eventually students) to express their feelings and emotions by using "I" statements. This shifts the dynamic of the conversation away from accusatory "you" statements that can leave the other person feeling defensive. This simple change can develop empathy because the technique shifts the discussion from talking *to* students to talking *with* them. Adding an "I" statement, then, is a way for you to voice your feelings and allow students an opportunity to respond.

When teachers use "I" statements and provide background, students are better able to grasp what the teacher wants. These interactions are private and do not rely on public humiliation to control behavior. For example, placing your hand on a shoulder and quietly stating, "Taylor, it's hard for me to give good directions when you're talking at the same time," is likely going to be enough to redirect the behavior as an empathetic response, rather than temporary compliance. When the goal is behavioral compliance, demanding attention may work, at least temporarily. But students do not develop empathy when they are just told to obey. Conversations like this can change the narrative as student and teacher consider the other person's perspective.

Relationship Repair

It is inevitable that relationships with teachers and peers will sometimes be strained, and students have to learn how to repair relationships when that happens. Not only does this create a more conducive learning environment, it is also a healthy habit to develop for life outside the classroom. Of course, there have to be growth-producing relationships in the first place for students to learn to repair. When students have positive, healthy relationships with adults, they are much more willing to work to repair those relationships when damaged.

The most powerful tool we can recommend for teachers who want to integrate a focus on relationship repair into their day-to-day practice is the impromptu conversation. It is a major shift in thinking for educators to consider that problematic student behavior is less about the rules being broken and more about the relationships that have been violated. Impromptu conversations allow teachers to mobilize their skills, using "I" statements in a more extended way. This process is useful when a teacher wants to address minor infractions within the classroom that are not significant enough to require administrative support. When teachers lack tools to address such concerns and must instead ask administrators to deal with even minor problems, students do not develop empathy for their teachers or anyone else in the classroom. When administrators "steal the conflict," swooping in to solve the problem for the teacher, they rob teachers of a chance to invest in the relationship with the student. When it is the administrator doing the quick fix, it is often a quick assignment of blame, a correction, and a generic promise to try to behave better. Even more problematic is that the student never had an opportunity to understand how his or her actions affected others—and the teacher could have used the conflict to teach students how to go about repairing relationships. Of course, there are times when the actions are serious enough to warrant administrative intervention. But we're talking about low-level problematic behavior that can be changed when students see that their teachers take control of the situation and address it proactively.

At the school where we work, administrators and teachers work together to make these impromptu conversations possible. Teachers can request coverage in the classroom by an administrator so that they can step out into the hallway with the student. Once there, the teacher uses "I" statements to explain the concern and solicits dialogue from the student, as in the following example:

Teacher: What was happening just now? I noticed that you've got your head down on the table.

Student: I'm just not feeling it today.

Teacher: Hmm, that's a problem. I've got some good stuff planned, but I can see you're not with me. What needs to happen to get you back to where you need to be? I can usually count on you.

Student: It's just I'm falling behind in my classes. I don't know how I can catch up.

Teacher: I'm glad you told me. You're up-to-date in here, but I didn't know about your other classes. We can't solve this right now, but can you meet me at lunch? We can make a plan.

Student: Sure. Thanks.

Teacher: Let's get back in there so we can get back to talking about the Progressive Era. I'll ask Rico to share his notes from class this morning so you get up to speed.

Impromptu conversations like this can head off conflicts before they damage the relationship between student and teacher.

Conflicts of a more serious nature require more than an impromptu conversation and usually involve an administrator or counselor, as well as the student's family. But current approaches can leave something to be desired. When children misbehave, adults are notorious for asking, "Why did you do that?" It practically begs the student to say, "I don't know." Sometimes, especially with younger students, they really *don't* know. There are better questions to ask. For example, starting with "What happened?" makes it harder for a student to answer that they don't know what happened. When we ask *what* happened, we are opening the door for them to share *their* perspective. Following the "what happened" question, we often use a scripted conversation with the offender (adapted from Costello, Wachtel, & Wachtel, 2009) that includes the following questions:

- What were you thinking about at the time?
- What have you thought about since?
- Who's been affected by what you've done, in what ways?
- What do you think you might need to do to make things right? (p. 16)

Having this type of conversation can help determine if the student is ready to make amends and restore the relationship. We aren't suggesting that a single conversation will address the harm done; it really depends on the severity of the violation. There may be a series of actions required to restore the relationship. In addition, there may be further consequences, such as loss of privileges, detention, or suspension. But it is vital to include restoration and making amends as part of the disciplinary process.

We follow a similar script to talk with the victim, whether student or adult. In traditional school disciplinary actions, the victim is an afterthought, simply told, "I'll take care of this. You can go back to class now." That sends a powerful and damaging message to victims—namely that they will need to deal with the hurt by themselves. The script we use to discuss the harm caused to a victim is also from Costello and colleagues (2009):

- What did you think when you realized what had happened?
- What effect has this incident had on you and others?
- What has been the hardest thing for you?
- What do you think needs to happen to make things right? (p. 16)

These conversations are separate and private, and are not conducted simultaneously. At some point, when the victim and offender are both ready, they need to make amends. If you have ever been in trouble, you know the hardest thing to do is to apologize and take responsibility for your actions. Dominique remembers growing up hearing his parents say that a conflict with his sister wasn't over until he took responsibility and apologized. He never wanted to say he was sorry, but it wasn't because he never regretted his behavior; he just didn't want to go through the difficult and awkward process of owning up to the fact that he wasn't his best self for a period of time. But apologizing and making it right is the reason that Dominique and his sister are still close today. Similar processes need to happen in school systems so that, when infractions occur, educators can help individuals take responsibility, apologize, and develop a plan to move forward with the repair. This process should be in place for student-to-student, teacher-to-student, teacher-to-teacher, and teacher-to-leader relationships. Remember, restorative practices are used so that

- Victims have a voice.
- Offenders take responsibility for their actions.
- All can start changing their behavior.

Takeaways

Teaching students social skills, communication skills, and empathy facilitates their ability to form and maintain relationships with others. These skills also are instrumental to developing the altruistic and responsible young people we need to foster a public spirit (see Chapter 6). Relationships are important for many reasons, including the fact that they result in productive interactions between people and make life more enjoyable. In fact, most people say that the relationships they have with others are among the most valuable things in their lives. But we invariably strain relationships and need to know how to repair those relationships.

QUESTIONS FOR REFLECTION

1. Do students in your school have strong social relationships (with their teachers, with one another, with themselves, and with the school)?
2. What communication skills do your students need to develop to improve their relationships with others?
3. Have you practiced circles, affective statements, and impromptu conversations? How could you use these tools to improve communication and relationships?
4. What role does empathy development play in your classroom? How (or how else) could you develop empathy in your students?
5. What do you do to help students learn to repair relationships that are damaged?
6. How could you more intentionally infuse existing collaborative learning routines with SEL elements to foster relationships between students?

CHAPTER 6

Public Spirit

Respect for others | Courage
Ethical responsibility | Civic responsibility
Social justice | Service learning | Leadership

Students at Randolph Middle School are gearing up for student government elections. Each fall, the student body selects representatives from each grade level, two at-large members, and an executive committee composed of a president, vice president, treasurer, and secretary. Valeria Guzmán-Sánchez has been the faculty advisor for student government for nine years. As a social studies teacher and coach of the school's debate team, she is passionate about her investment in the civic lives of her students. The school is in a border community between the United States and Mexico, and a number of students in the school are undocumented. "The notion of elections can get pretty mixed up when you're not able to vote in this country," said Ms. Guzmán-Sánchez. "We have to educate our students on what voting means for any community, including our own school community."

Under her guidance, candidates create platform statements about their position on school issues, including discipline and student voice in decision making. Each also proposes a school or community project. "None of this business about promising ice cream at lunch," Ms. Guzmán-Sánchez chuckled. "I want them to clearly understand they are servant-leaders, not a monarchy." Students interested in running for office must first prepare a plan for candidacy.

Therese, a candidate for 8th grade representative, met with Ms. Guzmán-Sánchez to shape her plans. Therese noted that she supported the school's shift to restorative practices but wanted to see more student involvement in the process. "I think we should have a student panel formed to be a part of the [discipline] process," she explained. Ms. Guzmán-Sánchez agreed, but she also pushed Therese to consider the details further: "Who would be on this panel?" When Therese replied that it would be representatives from student government, the teacher challenged her. "That's concentrating a lot of influence in a few hands," Ms. Guzmán-Sánchez said. "How might you broaden this to involve a wider number of students?"

Over the next 10 minutes, Therese fleshed out her platform on the issue with the guidance of Ms. Guzmán-Sánchez. Several weeks later, she presented as part of her campaign speech a proposal that the elected student government commission a work group to survey constituents about a possible student restorative practices panel and then meet with school leaders to discuss limitations and possibilities. The formation and composition of the group would be determined by the student body after a full plan had been presented to them. "I'm giving us a deadline of January to present the plan to all of you," Therese said. "I don't just speak for change. I *make* change."

Needless to say, Therese was elected.

Throughout our students' school careers, mindful educators prompt them to learn about themselves, both who they are and who they want to become. In Therese's final statement, we see evidence of her identity and agency: she's a changemaker. When we look at the work she did to confront a problem and think through possible solutions, we see evidence of cognitive regulation. But Therese's willingness to take school government so seriously—to move beyond what is often reduced to a popularity contest—was nurtured by the structures and expectations developed by Ms. Guzmán-Sánchez and her predecessors. Years ago, staff at Randolph Middle School set out to shape student government as an instrument for student empowerment, and they used the platform expectations to set a tone for servant leadership and public spirit.

Our society is continuously shaped and redefined by the people who live in this democracy, and its endurance depends on each generation's ability and willingness to engage in civil discourse. Education is critical to this endeavor, but it's more than just academic knowledge—of government, economics, politics, the legal system, science, logic, and reasoning—that matters. Social and emotional learning is an under-the-radar essential. From parents, families, their communities—and yes, their teachers—students either learn or fail to learn how to monitor their emotions, self-regulate, and exhibit prosocial behaviors, especially in complicated times.

Public Spirit Defined

We define *public spirit* as active interest and personal investment in the well-being of one's communities. Those "communities" include home, school, neighborhood, state or province, region, country, and the world. By including public spirit in our model of social and emotional learning (SEL), we hope to underscore the outward-facing aspects of SEL and amplify the growing appreciation of how these skills influence every corner of our society.

The National Commission on Social, Emotional, and Academic Development at the Aspen Institute consists of 25 members from education, research, policy, business, and the military. In its 2018 policy document, the Commission stated that a primary goal is for students to accept "their responsibility to take an active role in their communities and contribute to civic life" and further see "the integration of social, emotional, and academic development as the pathway to learning that achieves these ends" (Berman et al., 2018, p. 4).

So that's public spirit roughly defined; let's take a moment to consider its real-life expression. The spring of 2018 marked a watershed moment in the lives of many young people. Propelled by a school shooting at a Florida high school, which joined a long list of other such events that have rocked the nation over the last two decades, students raised their voices in protest against gun violence. We know that the politicized landscape provoked passionate responses regarding gun control and Second Amendment rights. Regardless of what you believe about the Second Amendment, consider the civic engagement of a group of high school students. They took public action to present their views in articulate and nonviolent ways. Savvy communicators, these student organizers used social media to distribute information and coordinate voter registration drives, walkouts, and protests. They leveraged their First Amendment rights to free speech and peaceful assembly. And they endured criticism and engaged in public debate. We are reminded that some of America's "founding fathers" were about the age of these students. For example, on July 4, 1776, the Marquis de Lafayette was 18, James Monroe was 18, Alexander Hamilton was 21, and Sybil Ludington ("the female Paul Revere") was 15. In other words, young people have been civically engaged in the United States since the country was formed. In fact, Thomas Jefferson (age 33 when he drafted the Declaration of Independence) is known for saying, "An educated citizenry is a vital requisite for our survival as a free people."

All this to say, what we teach students in school matters. Lithwick (2018) credits "the power of a comprehensive education" for the Parkland students' activism, further noting,

> Students who were being painstakingly taught about drama, media, free speech, political activism, and forensics became the epicenter of the school-violence crisis and handled it creditably . . . . Extracurricular education—one that focuses on skills beyond standardized testing and rankings—creates passionate citizens who are spring-loaded for citizenship. (¶9)

Children and adolescents develop public spirit through respect for self and others, which goes hand in hand with understanding the ethical responsibilities of membership in their communities. Perseverance in the face of challenging problems is crucial for public spirit, as societal problems are not easily fixed. Principles of justice should be applied fairly and courageously. Community service and service learning are woven into academic experiences. Finally, fostering student leadership helps students find their voice.

This is our payoff as a society. We need the next generation of leaders to chart a course that is humane and growth producing. What they need from us is to learn the SEL skills that are infused in public spirit in order to live and work together. These skills can act upon values in the face of challenges to "pursue the positive difference they can make in the world" (Berman et al., 2018, p. 4). Yet the current status of civic engagement among adults is startling and disheartening. According to the briefings at the Democracy at a Crossroads National Summit (Levine & Kawashima-Ginsberg, 2017) and others (e.g., Desliver, 2016; Kristian, 2014),

- Thirty-five percent of millennials (born between 1981 and 1996) said they were losing faith in American democracy, and just 25 percent were confident in the democratic system.
- Twenty-four percent of U.S. millennials considered democracy to be a "bad" or "very bad" way of running the country.
- Only one in four Americans can name the three branches of government, but 75 percent can name an *American Idol* judge.
- Four out of five Americans think incivility and political dysfunction prevent our nation from moving forward.
- Only about 29 percent of eligible Americans participated in the 2016 primary elections that determined the major party nominees.

Not all students seem poised to assume civic leadership, at least according to one respected measure: the 2014 8th grade National Assessment of Educational Progress (NAEP; U.S. Department of Education, 2015). Scores for civic education were dismal, with only 23 percent of students reaching proficiency. This stands in stark contrast with the comments of Justice Sandra Day O'Connor, who has noted, "As a citizen, you need to know how to be a part of [the civil process], how to express yourself—not just vote" (Gergen, 2012).

A major outcome from investing in SEL might just be the development of civic dispositions and civic skills that result in civic action. Classrooms are major forums for doing just that, as teachers bring together the emotional, cognitive, and prosocial skills students need in school and in life. As we have asserted throughout this book, these skills are intertwined and cannot be restricted to a weekly 45-minute lesson.

Many of the topics in this chapter are traditionally associated with character education. However, "character is plural" (Park, Tsukayama, Goodwin,

Patrick, & Duckworth, 2017, p. 17) and includes the intrapersonal, interpersonal, and cognitive dispositions "to act, think, and feel in ways that benefit the individual and society" (p. 16). This chapter is therefore about taking action to contribute positively to one's family, classroom, and larger community.

Respect for Others

The heart of public spirit is respect for others. This is more than "tolerance," which implies that you are pushing aside disapproval in an effort to endure the existence of others. Respect for others entails seeing worth and value in every human life, regardless of differences. Further, those who respect others recognize that collective strength is derived from differences, not just similarities. It is an assertion of the rights of others. Empathy (see Chapter 5) is crucial in respect for others, as it requires a caring stance. Noddings (2012) calls this the *ethics of caring*, but she cautions that too often empathy is rooted in comparing one's feelings to the situations of others. Consider how often we ask children, "How would *you* feel if that happened to you?" as if the primary yardstick is to first consider themselves. "But the empathy of care ethics is other-oriented, not self-oriented," says Nodding, reminding us that true empathy lies in carefully listening to others in order to hear their thoughts and feelings (p. 771).

Empathy without respect for others can rapidly devolve into an inflated sense of privilege, which is damaging because it divides rather than unites. For instance, disability simulations in which a participant temporarily encounters a disability (e.g., being blindfolded, using a wheelchair) have been widely criticized for being inauthentic activities, as the emphasis is solely on sensory loss rather than a lived experience. There are other unintended consequences associated with disability simulations. Some participants report that they are primarily grateful *they* don't have a disability, which contributes to social distancing. In addition, post-simulation surveys completed by participants reflect a reduced belief in the competence of a person with a disability (Cuddy, Fiske, & Glick, 2007).

When Monica, a student with intellectual disability, was enrolled in her class, 4th grade teacher Leah Katz knew that she needed to ensure that membership, empathy, and respect were a part of the social fabric of the classroom community. This was the first year Monica had been in a general education classroom, and she didn't know anyone. Over the course of several months, Ms. Katz infused SEL principles into content lessons. None ever addressed disability by name; instead, they focused on appreciating and understanding differences. For instance, students being given instruction on narrative writing used descriptive language to write about the unique physical properties of an apple they were given, then were challenged to identify their personal apple when it was placed in a basket with a dozen others. In math, they surveyed their families about their potato preparation preferences (e.g., mashed, baked), then graphed the collective results using histograms. Through these and other SEL-infused lessons, the focus was first on the academic learning, and then on the ways they understood themselves and their classroom community. Over the course of the year, Ms. Katz witnessed friendships with Monica emerging, including invitations for activities outside school such as birthday parties and movies. Most of all, she noticed "a strong sense of responsible citizenship developing in many of the students . . . . Questions about culture, language, ethnicity, perceived ability, and gender were asked with interest and respect" (Katz, Sax, & Fisher, 2003, p. 10). It is within these transactions that respect for others is fostered.

Older students are challenged by a 24/7 news cycle that seems bent on profiling the profound disrespect some have for fellow humans. Middle and high school students need space to be able to address and process current events using a set of agreed-upon core values and ethics. Eighth grade science teacher Katie Basilone begins each year with the same set of norms we profiled in Chapter 5. She uses these to frame what occurs inside her classroom and in the larger world:

- Take care of yourself.
- Take care of each other.
- Take care of this place.

"I use these as a springboard for us to talk about a whole variety of things," she said. "Put away the lab equipment? *Take care of this place.* Study your notes before the test? *Take care of yourself.* Contribute to your group's discussion? *Take care of each other.*" But there are times when outside events intrude on instruction and need to be addressed. Referring to a violent crime that occurred in the community where they live, Ms. Basilone said, "We needed to talk about what had happened. Members of rival gangs had a series of confrontations over a few days, and a young person died. Some said it was about *respect.* When I heard that, I knew we needed to unpack that notion."

Using a communication circle (see Chapter 5), the class discussed what had occurred using the three statements. "We started with defining *place* as our neighborhood, and what respect means for a community," she explained. Working backwards from there, they debated definitions of respect for others and respect for self:

> It wasn't an easy conversation. They're 13 years old, and several of them are connected through family or friends to the events that happened. But we had to get our minds wrapped around what respect is, as well as disrespect. Most of all, we talked about our personal responsibilities.

Ms. Basilone's colleague, 8th grade English teacher Mikhail Graber, continued the conversation in his classes. "I wanted us to read and discuss a book as a classroom community," he said, "one that could open up the topic about making decisions based on hard ethical choices, instead of just following the crowd." However, Mr. Graber did not want to select a book that had overt connections to gangs. Instead, he chose *Wringer* (Spinelli, 1996). This allegory is about a town that celebrates the killing of pigeons each year, and a protagonist who does not want to participate. Palmer reaches the age of 10, when boys are expected to be "wringers" who run onto the field to wring the necks of pigeons that have been shot but have not yet died. He is faced with pressure from peers and the legacy of a father who was considered to be one of the great wringers. However, when Palmer adopts a pigeon of his own as a secret pet, he grows resolute in his resistance of societal pressures about this rite of passage. "The dialogue has been great," said the English teacher. "They have drawn parallels to the gang life and Palmer's ethical dilemma." The class finished the book with a Socratic seminar framed by the three norms drawn from Ms. Basilone's science class: *What are the challenges of taking care of oneself, each other, and this place in* Wringer? *In our own lives?*

Both teachers commented on the power of a common language of respect. "Our community has been rocked by this event, and we would be doing a huge disservice to our students to pretend it didn't happen," said Ms. Basilone. "I've been able to broaden concepts of respect to include things like our environment." Mr. Graber added, "I'm seeing more nuanced definitions of *respect* in student essays. That word gets tossed around so much, but it usually means *intimidation*. They're seeing it's a lot more complicated. I'm getting them to think."

Courage

Courage is persistence in the face of fear (Norton & Weiss, 2009). It is a behavior or action rather than an innate disposition, and therefore it manifests itself differently depending on the circumstance. Courageous actions draw on many of the elements discussed elsewhere in this book, including a sense of resilience, the capacity to cope, a positive sense of agency and identity, and a host of prosocial behaviors (Hannah, Sweeney, & Lester, 2010). Courage is exhibited when someone takes on a meaningful goal even though there is personal risk—and these risks are often psychological or social, rather than physical. Courageous acts include speaking up on behalf of others and making unpopular choices that are nonetheless ethical.

Fifth grade teacher Therese Pelletier uses a literature circle format (Daniels, 2002) to explore expressions of courage in the lives of young people. She previews each book, then asks students to list their top two choices. Using their responses, she recently created literature circles for five novels:

- *Esperanza Rising* (Ryan, 2000)
- *Number the Stars* (Lowry, 1989)
- *The True Confessions of Charlotte Doyle* (Avi, 1990)
- *The Crossover* (Alexander, 2015)
- *Wonder* (Palacio, 2012)

Ms. Pelletier explained that she tries to present a range of literature that transcends historical and contemporary settings. "Courage is an enduring quality," she said. Students meet twice a week to discuss the portion of the text they agreed to read. After discussing literary aspects such as plot analysis, they turn their attention to the subject of courage, using a few guiding questions (McConnell, 2011, p. 65) to frame their discussion: *Where does courage come from? How can an act of courage affect others? How are risk-taking and courage related? How are endurance and courage related?*

Seventh grade English teacher Kelvin Parker's curriculum standards include formal presentations, and he uses one of these as a reason for students to investigate courage. Each year, he asks his students to consult the lists of individuals awarded the military Congressional Medal of Honor or the Nobel Peace Prize, and investigate, select one person to study, and prepare a written report on how that person exhibited courage in the face of fear. "Then," Mr. Parker told us, "I have them select a second person to study—a *civilian* Congressional Medal of Honor winner who exemplifies a similar kind of courage."

The civilian Congressional Medal of Honor is presented annually to individuals and organizations in four categories: single acts of heroism, service acts, community service hero, and the Young Hero Award for those between the ages of 8 and 17. The students' formal presentation is an analytical comparison of the two people selected. Mr. Parker explained:

> It's easy to see how a towering figure like Martin Luther King Jr. is courageous, or how war heroes like Gary Gordon and Randall Shughart, who sacrificed their lives to save others in the Battle of Mogadishu, were courageous. But it's also intimidating. They think to themselves, "I could never do that." I want them to see how "ordinary" people are courageous. The truth is, there's nothing ordinary about these people *or* about my students. I want them to see the extraordinary in others and in themselves.

We don't want students to think that courage is a trait manifested only in others, or that courage is exclusively about putting one's life on the line for somebody else. Every day, ordinary people quietly use grit and determination to make their corner of the world a better place. Therefore, we return to perseverance and grit in this chapter on public spirit in order to explore its relationship to how we interact with the world. The ability to take on a community issue is a courageous decision, and one that typically requires perseverance and grit on the part of the person leading change. Schools around the country have engaged their students with scheduled time to explore new ideas through Genius Hour and makerspaces. Genius Hour was inspired by Google's commitment to protect 20 percent of their engineers' time to work on projects of interest to them. There was a payoff for the organization, too, as innovations that originated from the 80/20 program evolved into Google News and Gmail. Although the 80/20 program was discontinued at Google in 2013, the program inspired educational applications for students to innovate. Makerspaces are another outgrowth of this effort. Schools and libraries around the country fill labs with 3-D printers, software, electronics, and other hardware to support STEM efforts and give students time and space to be able to explore their passions.

It takes perseverance and grit to aid others when problems are not easily solved, and it also takes time. Genius Hour and makerspace efforts should include expectations that the projects address ways to aid others. Students at Hendricks Middle School submit proposals for Genius Hour projects that include a rationale for how their exploration will benefit others. "All projects require teacher approval," said Aleesa Lincoln-Dwyer. "Last year we added another criterion to the proposal rubric that the student include a benefit statement. How might this investigation benefit someone else?" Ms. Lincoln-Dwyer said that the benefit requirement was challenging for students at first, who typically used Genius Hour to explore their own interests. "We want them to consider how their learning might make someone else's life better." They read *The Boy Who Harnessed the Wind* (Kamkwamba & Mealer, 2010) and watched William Kamkwamba's TED Talks about his work. "We discussed how William linked his passion for science with a need to improve the lives of his family and village." She said that her students commented that William's use of the library and scrap materials wasn't all that different from the way their Genius Hours were staged.

"That was a turning point," said the teacher. Looking around the library, she pointed to students who were working on rockets ("Because our space program needs people like me to get us to Mars"), the prison system ("There are too many people from my neighborhood who end up there, and they don't learn any skills"), and hydroponics ("Lots of hungry people and climate change are going to change the way we farm"). Ms. Lincoln-Dwyer also noted that the complexity of projects has increased. "Last year we had proposals on how to make slime and how to develop better skills in soccer. Not that they weren't worthwhile, but most of the projects were focused on their lives only," she said. "With this year's projects, students answer one question but then have three new ones to address. It's been great to see 6th and 7th graders discovering their own level of commitment to complicated issues."

Ethical Responsibility

"It's not fair!" How many times have you heard that from your students? Issues of fairness are particularly vexing for children. Broadening their focus from their own needs to include the needs of others is not easy. But ethical responsibility requires that students merge their own circumstances with those of the group. Fairness without contemplation of the effect on the group is selfishness. Further, ethically responsible decisions sometimes require judgments about right and wrong, as well as accepting responsibility for one's actions. An ethically responsible person acts in a way that is honorable and principled. In previous chapters, we discussed these concepts through the lens of prosocial behaviors (e.g., helping, sharing, teamwork). Here we expand the scope to include the public spirit element *community harmony*.

In education circles, the moral and ethical development of children and young adults is often discussed using Kohlberg's (1963) stage theory (see Figure 6.1). Very young children operate primarily at the pre-conventional stage, making judgments strictly from an egocentric perspective. (For a vivid illustration of the egocentric perspective, watch a couple of 2-year-olds with one toy between them.) As children move into preschool and primary grades, they enter the conventional moral reasoning stage, with all of those squabbles about fairness. As educators, we create the conditions that influence how and how quickly children and adolescents proceed through these stages. In terms of moral reasoning, young people can generally operate one level up from their current stage, but typically no higher. Therefore, it would be futile to expect that a child in a Stage 3 level would be able to operate at a Stage 5 level (which is the rationale behind a democracy). But at Stage 3, they can be stretched to a Stage 4, also a bedrock of democracy.

FIGURE 6.1
Kohlberg's Stages of Moral Development

	Stage	What Drives Decisions	Limitation
Pre-Conventional	Stage 1: Driven by obedience and punishment	"It's bad to do that because I got punished."	Little sense of right or wrong
	Stage 2: Driven by self-interest	"What's in it for me?"	Does not consider perspective of others
Conventional	Stage 3: Driven by conformity to social standards	"I am a good boy" or "I am a good girl"	Emergence of social consensus to govern behavior, but not necessarily an internal compass
	Stage 4: Driven by social obedience	"Rules and laws maintain the social order."	Morality is primarily determined by a society
Post-Conventional	Stage 5: Driven by the social contract	"All people have rights and hold differing values and opinions."	Decisions reached through compromise, based on the greatest good for the greatest number of people
	Stage 6: Driven by universal ethical principles	"Laws must be grounded in justice, and unjust laws must be disobeyed."	Doubtful that anyone consistently is at this level

Ethical responsibility evolves across a lifetime, and as adults we face experiences that shape our perspectives and beliefs. However, young people profit from first encountering ethical dilemmas in text and multimedia. The struggles of characters, real and imagined, as they wrestle with determining what is fair, what is right, and what it means to accept responsibility can light a path for students to follow when confronted with similar problems in their own lives. The raja must confront his own unfair treatment of his people in *One Grain of Rice* (Demi, 1997). David has to own his mistakes in *David Gets in Trouble* (Shannon, 2002). Throughout the *Hunger Games* book trilogy (Collins, 2008) and films (Jacobson & Ross, 2012), Katniss Everdeen deals with an evolving sense of right and wrong in a dystopian world. Ponyboy must accept responsibility for his role in the deaths of two people in *The Outsiders* (Hinton, 1967).

The 1st graders in Thom Reeves's class explored ethical responsibility through discussion of the picture book *A Bike Like Sergio's* (Boelts, 2016). The story concerns a young boy named Ruben, who finds a $100 bill on his way to the store and the ethical dilemma he faces about whether to return it or keep the money to purchase a new bicycle. He is also plagued with the knowledge that his mother could use the money to buy groceries the family needs. Ruben later gives back the money to the woman who lost it but remarks, "I am happy and mixed up, full and empty, with what's right and what's gone."

During the discussion that followed the class's interactive read-aloud, Mr. Reeves returned to this sentence and asked his students to tell him about Ruben's conflicting feelings and decision. Then he recorded their insights on two language charts. One featured the words *happy*, *full*, and *what's right*; the other, the words *mixed up*, *empty*, and *what's gone*. "They really had to grapple with these ideas, first in looking for evidence in the story about both sides of Ruben's dilemma, and then their own opinions," Mr. Reeves told us. "Not all of them were convinced that Ruben's decision was the one they would make. But I create chances for us to have these debates so they can explore their own thinking."

Eighth grade social studies teacher Jill Ammon uses the preambles of the U.S. Declaration of Independence and Constitution to examine ethics and morality at the birth of a democracy. "Both of these are foundational documents. I've found that an interesting way to make them stick is to have students analyze the ethics behind natural rights and inalienable rights," she said. "The conversation really takes off when I challenge them to reconsider these ideals in a system that allowed slavery to exist for another 90 years." She notes that this examination of the influence of ethical responsibility in our nation's founding is vital for young adolescents. "They are in that stage in their lives where they are beginning to perceive that everything isn't as easy as 'right or wrong,'" Mrs. Ammon told us. "The ambiguity that lies between ideals and actions can be tough to handle. The social contract that these documents convey also created gaps for those who didn't have a voice, especially women and enslaved people."

Civic Responsibility

In addition to the ethical responsibility to conduct oneself in ways that are honorable and principled, members of society are charged with being involved in community improvement. This civic responsibility is the mark of a participatory democracy that seeks to give voice to all and to address social injustices. The dispositions and skills fostered through emotional and cognitive regulation (see Chapters 3 and 4), as well as prosocial behaviors (Chapter 5), are expressed in broader measure in local, national, and global communities. The principles that have marked the founding of democracies throughout the world rest on the notion that the people are empowered to make decisions. Consider the definition of a *republic*: "a government in which supreme power resides in a body of citizens entitled to vote and is exercised by elected officers and representatives responsible to them and governing according to law" (*Merriam-Webster Online*, n.d.).

U.S. history teacher Kendra Marcus uses a diary entry from James McHenry, a Maryland delegate at the 1787 convention that eventually yielded the U.S. Constitution (see Potter, 2016), to build her students' sense of civic responsibility. The entry from September 18, 1787, recounts a conversation

he witnessed between Benjamin Franklin and a woman on the street as he
exited the meeting:

> a lady asked Dr. Franklin
> well Doctor what we got
> a republic or a monarchy—
> A republic replied the Doctor
> if you can keep it.

"I introduce this in the first week of school, and it becomes a core
theme for the entire course," said Ms. Marcus. "Preserving the principle that
the people, not a king, make decisions means that we all must be actively
engaged in the national dialogue." Her school serves a significant number of
students who have emigrated from other countries, including some who are
not documented.

> I know there are a lot of politics involved, and some of my students are
> demoralized by issues of citizenship and the rhetoric surrounding it. But
> I want them to see that their civic responsibilities transcend documents.
> Especially at the local level, they have the ability to do so much good.

Throughout the course, Ms. Marcus returns frequently to Franklin's
challenge that retaining a republic requires active pursuit. Her students
examine moments of crisis using history as a lens. She explained:

> The Missouri Compromise, the forced displacement of native peoples, the
> abolitionist movement, the struggle for women's rights, the Progressive
> Era, the civil rights movement . . . all of these were times when those who
> answered the call of civic responsibility did so whether they were citizens
> with voting rights or not.

She added, "Franklin's words are a touchstone for us. They are a call to
action. But it's up to us to decide if we answer."

A simple way to foster civic responsibility among the youngest students is to encourage them to take pride in and care for their classroom

environment. Preschool and primary teachers establish routines for their students for cleaning up the workspace, returning materials, and pushing in chairs. Many teachers rotate classroom jobs so that every student experiences the responsibility and pride of a job well done and its effect on the classroom community. First grade teacher Leyna Romero displays a chart of classroom jobs with student names assigned to each. In addition to expected ones like Line Leader and Door Holder, she includes those that benefit the entire classroom in more prominent ways. "One of the jobs I assign is the Directions Director," said Ms. Romero. "That person repeats the directions I give for the whole group and, if the directions are confusing, asks me clarifying questions. It's kind of like being the spokesperson." She also appoints a person each week to serve as the classroom greeter. "We get lots of visitors, so the greeter welcomes the person, explains what it is we're doing, and helps them find a seat in the room." She uses other jobs to build civic responsibility, including the Green Team, who make sure the recyclable can is filled with the correct items, the lights are turned off when the room is empty, and any compostable waste is taken to the school's composting station. Another classroom job is Tech Support, making sure the computer carts are locked and plugged in to recharge overnight.

Students also learn about the consequences of voting while in school. In Katrina Ortega's 4th grade class, students vote on many things, big and small. For example, they vote on class read-alouds following a brief teacher introduction to two books on a related topic, on assessment types, and on class representatives. Students have time to share their thinking before the class votes. For example, Winston, a student in the class, wanted to have math first thing in the morning rather than after reading and language arts. He asked Ms. Ortega, "Can we vote on this? Or did you already decide, and it's not something we can vote on?" Ms. Ortega assured Winston that a vote was reasonable and said that there should be some discussion about the order of the curriculum before there was a class vote. They agreed that there would be a vote the following Monday and that students would be invited to share their thinking for 10 minutes after lunch each day before the vote. Many of the students had specific reasons for either wanting the schedule to stay the same or for changing it. As Ms. Ortega reminded them, "Any time there is a vote, there is a risk of some people being disappointed. We are a community, so we have to be sensitive to the feelings of people who lose the election as well." The class ended up voting and the curriculum was changed. As one of the students who did not vote to change it said, "It's OK. I mean we're still learning. I like math after recess, but it's fine this way, really."

Middle school teachers Samuel French and Lindsey Farentino use the online game program iCivics (www.icivics.org), which was first conceived by Justice Sandra Day O'Connor. This free resource has 19 different games, plus 150 lesson plans for teachers. Ms. Farentino told us,

> As English and history teachers, we want our students to master standards in both areas. The games that they have in this program develop literacy skills and civic skills at the same time. My students especially love the game Do I Have a Right? [in which student-lawyers decide whether a client has a constitutionally sound case], but we play all of the games. We also use the recommended teacher format, where we teach and introduce a lesson before students play the game and then have lessons after.

Independent research suggests that the iCivics curriculum works. For example, using the curriculum improved students' civics scores by 37 percent (LeCompte, Moore, & Blevins, 2011) In addition, students' writing skills increased when teachers implemented iCivics (Kawashima-Ginsberg, 2012). And perhaps even more important, the outcomes in both studies were equitable across gender, race/ethnicity, and socioeconomic status.

The high school history teachers at the school where we work host debates every three weeks or so. The students and faculty agree on the topics, and teams prepare. For the first debate of the school year, students draw cards, pro or con, and the teacher assigns them to groups. Although students have some time in class to prepare for the debate, they have to do a lot of the research outside class. As students' debating skills strengthen, the preassigned roles of pro and con are eliminated. By the end of the first semester, they must prepare arguments for both sides, as they will not learn to which side they are assigned until the day of the debate. That day, groups draw numbers and places and debate against teams from other classes (e.g., a 9th grade team might debate an 11th grade team). Our students are very proud of their debate skills and they are thrilled when the judges announce winners. But, as one of our colleagues said,

> It's really not about winning, per se. It's civic action and responsibility. It's about learning and thinking, and considering both sides of a topic. And we think that our students will be more prepared to engage in public discourse and debate as adults because of the skills we've given them in class.

Social Justice

Acting in the public spirit is driven by a sense of social justice. The human rights of all people grounds the work of teaching social justice to students. Justice is not vengeance, but rather the pursuit of material improvement in the quality of life of others. Much of the work of social justice is captured in the 30 rights for humans set forth in 1948 by the United Nations in response to the horrors of World War II. The Universal Declaration of Human Rights has since served as a foundational document for other declarations, including those for people with disabilities and for children. These universal rights include freedom of expression and thought, as well as freedom from want, torture, slavery, and oppression. Basic human rights are outlined as well, including those pertaining to food, water, shelter, and the right to move. Arguably most powerful are the last two: each person has a responsibility to other people to protect their rights and freedoms, and no one can take away your human rights.

Advocacy for others is an important SEL skill for children to acquire, and it is up to adults to show them how to go about it. Primary-age students are accustomed to being taken care of, rather than caring for others, so their sense of agency in this arena is not well developed. However, small people can make a big difference. Montgomery, Miller, Foss, Tallakson, and Howard (2017) described the efforts of a "mighty-hearted" kindergarten class who were energized by Article 26 of the United Nations declaration, which states that everyone has the right to an education. They read a variety of books as a class about the rights of children and the conditions under which some children live. The teacher collaborated with others to raise money for a middle school in a poor community in El Salvador so that students could continue their education beyond 6th grade. The kindergartners worked with an art professor and a printmaker to design banners that were sold to raise money for the school. Interviews with the children during and after the project revealed that they "recognized their own educational rights and privileges, as well as demonstrated a sense of care and empathy for their global peers" (p. 13).

High school chemistry teacher Clark Anderson uses *Every Human Has Rights* (National Geographic, 2008) to introduce the ethical responsibilities of the sciences to forward social justice for all. The photographic essay is a moving way to introduce the United Nations document and to frame subsequent discussions about ethics in the field. Dr. Anderson used two of the universal rights (i.e., Article 25 on a standard of living and Article 29 on the responsibility of all to protect the rights of others) to frame his teaching surrounding the water crisis in Flint, Michigan. In Flint, since 2014, more than 100,000 people have been exposed to lead in their drinking water. His students learned about efforts by scientists from Virginia Tech, the Environmental Protection Agency, and the Hurley Medical Center to chronicle exposure rates and lead poisoning's effects on children and adults.

Using published data, Dr. Anderson's chemistry students analyzed the reported findings and used GIS maps online to locate lead pipe zones. His students also investigated current efforts to mitigate the damage to children and critiqued efforts to curtail further harm. "An early lab experiment I did with them was to demonstrate why boiling lead-contaminated water does not reduce lead levels," the teacher explained. "We then looked at the efforts the city of Flint is taking to educate residents about proper handling of contaminated water." Dr. Anderson was clear on what he wants his students to know:

> Chemistry, journalism, medicine, education—all of these fields are filled with professionals who understand their responsibility in ensuring social justice is achieved. It takes courage and persistence, but without people who take this duty seriously, untold numbers of people can be harmed.

Service Learning

Use of *service learning*, an educational approach that melds academic learning with community well-being, has grown in popularity in the last decade. Service learning differs from *community service*, which is primarily enacted though individual volunteering. Although community service has value, it lacks the reciprocity that comes with service learning, wherein students become involved in organizations, "working with, not for," others (Boyle-Baise & Zevin, 2013, p. 217). Unlike community service, service learning is a collaborative partnership among the school, teachers, a community organization, and the student (National Youth Leadership Council [NYLC], 2008). Goals for a project are derived from specific content learning, with an emphasis on how concepts taught in the classroom come to life in a community setting. However, a danger of service learning is that it can devolve into a form of charity, "eliciting pity rather than prompting empathy for a disenfranchised group" (Strom, 2016, p. 37). Preparation is key to ensuring students have the cognitive, social, and emotional tools needed to understand their experiences and their agency.

The moniker of service learning has been attached to a range of out-of-school activities, even though many fail to meet the stated intent. A one-off experience such as serving food to the homeless just before Thanksgiving break is unlikely to have much of a lasting effect beyond pity and a social distancing of oneself from the problem ("I'm grateful that's not me"). The NYLC developed standards that address the reciprocal nature of service learning—a positive effect on the community and on the individual (NYLC, 2008):

- *Meaningful service.* Service learning actively engages participants in meaningful and personally relevant service activities.
- *Link to curriculum.* Service learning is intentionally used as an instructional strategy to meet learning goals or content standards.
- *Reflection.* Service learning incorporates multiple challenging reflection activities that are ongoing and that prompt deep thinking and analysis about oneself and one's relationship to society.

- *Diversity.* Service learning promotes understanding of diversity and mutual respect among all participants.
- *Youth voice.* Service learning provides youth with a strong voice in planning, implementing, and evaluating their experiences, with guidance from adults.
- *Partnerships.* Service learning partnerships are collaborative, are mutually beneficial, and address community needs.
- *Progress monitoring.* Service learning engages participants in an ongoing process to assess the quality of implementation and progress toward meeting specified goals, and uses results for improvement and sustainability.
- *Duration and intensity.* Service learning has sufficient duration and intensity to address community needs and meet specified outcomes.

Service learning is more commonly associated with high school and college students, although it is occurring with greater frequency with younger children. The kindergarten Banners for Books project described earlier is an example of service learning at the primary level. Service learning projects may be based at the school, for example, designing and tending a community garden to grow fresh vegetables and herbs for use in the school cafeteria. Fifth graders at Eagles Nest Elementary School who were studying nutrition worked with their school district food services department to identify what greens were needed, and collaborated with the facilities manager to identify an available plot on the school campus. One team of students met with a representative of the county cooperative extension program to consult on starting and sustaining a garden, choosing hardy varieties, and figuring out pest control. Another team worked with the school's parent-teacher organization to coordinate parent volunteers to aid in the construction of the garden. Students developed a maintenance schedule and rotated jobs weekly to water, weed, plant, and harvest during the school day. Since the initial development of the school community garden several years ago, subsequent classes have expanded its scope to include space and supplies for neighbors to plant their own vegetables.

The influence of civic engagement through service learning on academic achievement is strong, with an effect size of .58 (Hattie, 2009; see Chapter 1's discussion of effect sizes). Beyond academic learning, students participating in service learning projects—whether required or voluntary—report higher levels of motivation, autonomy, and self-determination after the experience (Kackar-Cam & Schmidt, 2014). Service learning is an expression of the many attributes taught through the integration of SEL in the curriculum. Through such experiences, students develop self-confidence and competency. After all, how do you know you are competent if you have never been put to the test? Students learn patience by delaying gratification (see Chapter 3), as meaningful projects aren't a quick fix. Cognitive regulation is also required, especially in setting goals and making decisions (see Chapter 4). Students must draw on prosocial skills and manage conflicts in order to advance the work (see Chapter 5). Finally, service learning fosters the kind of ethical and civic responsibilities we want all of our students to gain, as they see the power they have as individuals to make a difference. If you think we sound like fans of service learning, you're right.

Leadership

The development of engaged and inspired learners is an important outcome of social and emotional learning (Smith, Frey, Pumpian, & Fisher, 2017), but so is the development of engaging and inspiring leaders. We believe in helping every student find the leader within. We also believe that this doesn't necessarily have to involve the conventional structure of student leadership found in student government and clubs. Rather, we agree with Nelson (2017), who define *leadership* as "the process of helping people accomplish together what they would or could not as individuals" (p. 48).

When you think of student leaders, it's natural to have a pretty standard image in your mind of who they are: academically or athletically accomplished, well-spoken, and mature. But Nelson advises also identifying, developing, and deploying to do good work those students in your school whose potential is often overlooked because academic or behavioral challenges obscure their talents. He recommends (and we wholeheartedly endorse) consulting the Social Influence Survey (Nelson, 2009). This 25-item survey, which is available for free online, is focused on an individual child's behavior but targeted to adults. It asks questions about the degree to which peers seem to follow the child, whether the child seeks to negotiate deals, is viewed as "the class clown," and sticks to his or her principles even when others deviate. Note that the survey was written to zero in on problematic behaviors but these very same qualities, when properly channeled, will yield some of the very best student leaders.

Usually being number one a good thing, but leaders at Maryland's Marely Middle School were understandably distressed to find their school leading the country in number of school fights (Byland, 2015). When they examined their suspension and expulsion data, looking for trends, they found one particularly troubling trend: Students who were male, African American, and living in poverty were four times more likely to be suspended. The administration's response was to identify students who were "high flyers" on the suspension list and turn them into school leaders. They set up a leadership development program, built relationships with these students, provided them with additional academic support, and helped them develop impulse control and conflict resolution skills. Within one semester, Marley's suspension rates dropped significantly, and these students began to thrive. Over time, they did become school leaders—but first, the school taught them to lead themselves.

We believe schools must provide leadership opportunities beyond student government and offer a wider range of options for student participation. At the high school where we work, a group of students engage in service learning and leadership to design, host, and speak at an annual mental health conference for students from neighboring high schools. Other students at the school design a school conference called "A Day of Understanding" to promote dialogue among the student body. Students determine the content of the sessions and hire the keynote speakers. All the students in the school gather at the local convention center to spend the day listening to guests and their fellow students speak about issues of diversity. Last year, a student panel representing the world's major religions presented information on misconceptions about their faiths and the commonalities among them. Other speakers discussed issues surrounding gender expression, empowerment for people with disabilities, and self-determination. A third effort involves the entire student body in honing their leadership skills. Students transform every classroom in the school into a College and Career Symposium they host for families and the community one evening near the end of the school year. Classrooms are staffed by a team of students who explain their internship experiences (every student in grades 9–12 has an internship placement), and their occupational and educational aspirations. This effort is largely student-directed, with support from the entire school staff. The student teams must work together to plan the experience visitors will have in the room, order supplies, coordinate their schedules, and get feedback from the visitors. These mixed-age teams are challenged to resolve conflicts and come to consensus in order to present a polished product. Last year we hosted over 600 guests during the three-hour symposium.

Takeaways

The founding fathers of the United States believed that there were two ways to increase the likelihood that the democracy would last. The first was the division of the government into three branches willing to check and balance one another, and the second was education. They reasoned that survival of the democracy depended on an informed population who would engage in civic responsibility and civic action. And they believed that this learning could be acquired in school. We agree. Schools can be places where young people try out, and try on, their civic duties; where they learn about the government and what it means to them to participate in decision-making processes; and where they learn to advocate for what they believe as they learn to respect the rights of others.

QUESTIONS FOR REFLECTION

1. How much knowledge of civics do your students have?
2. Where are their opportunities in the curriculum to discuss ethical responsibility?
3. Is civic responsibility a focus, and do students have opportunities to engage in civic action, such as through debates, discussions, voting, and the like?
4. Is social justice a non-negotiable part of the classroom and school?
5. How could service learning transform SEL efforts at your school?
6. How do you cultivate leadership among your student body?

CHAPTER 7

Creating an SEL School

"Hope is not a plan."

Principal Shanika Bell was addressing the staff of the K–8 school she leads. Teachers and administrators at Bright Lights Leadership Academy had been interested in adopting an SEL program at their school. Several staff members had returned from a national conference, where they visited a number of booths to view curricular material. They were excited to share the brochures they gathered and speak about the relative advantages of each. "Some of these come with PD, too, so we can have a trainer come to our school," one teacher pointed out.

Dr. Bell listened carefully, then asked, "They all sound great in their own ways, but how do we know this is what we need?" After a few moments of silence, a teacher offered, "We hope this is going to be a good fit for our classrooms." That's when the principal said, "Hope is not a plan."

Dr. Bell then recounted past successes the school had experienced with other initiatives, such as developing communities of practice. "Now don't forget what we did to get us there. We looked at our data. We involved families in the decision making. And we set goals for ourselves. Shouldn't we stick with a decision-making approach that has worked for us?" The staff's hunches said that a social and emotional learning curriculum would aid them in moving students forward in their lives, but they agreed that, in their enthusiasm, they had overlooked some important steps. Dr. Bell was pleased with the direction of the discussion. "I agree that an SEL curriculum can be value-added. But we need to select the right one, make it our own, and infuse it into our daily practice, not just provide stand-alone lessons. So let's get to work. Who wants to lead a data work group? And we need some folks to work with gathering parent voices in this process."

The staff of Bright Lights Leadership Academy, with leadership from the principal, is enacting sound practices in school decision making. There are a variety of excellent SEL curricula available—but which is right for *your* school? How will these practices become part of the fabric of the school and not just something that is taught every Thursday afternoon? And how can home and community strengths be leveraged so that a fully integrated approach to social and emotional learning is realized?

Building SEL Capacity

The research is conclusive: SEL principles taught to students will not gain traction unless adults in the school can integrate them into daily practice and capitalize on real-life situations that demand their application (Jones et al., 2017).

The easy answer to building educators' SEL capacity is professional development (PD). But PD that lacks purpose is not effective. Isolated sessions that aren't linked to schoolwide agreements and resultant initiatives just aren't perceived as important and are unlikely to get the necessary buy-in. And without follow-up, including coaching and monitoring, even well-designed PD will wither in the face of competing demands.

SEL deserves to be anchored by every facet of school, including data systems, family engagement, and district goals. The only way to make that happen is through careful planning and pursuit of clear targets. Jones and colleagues (2018) suggest a four-stage approach:

1. Use data to guide decision making.
2. Include key stakeholders.
3. Identify needs and goals.
4. Select a program or approach based on goals.

We would further argue that it is a school staff's deliberate, collaborative engagement in this four-step process that will build the capacity necessary to make the effort successful. SEL integration is not a one-time thing, and neither is this four-step process. It's recursive and iterative, and schools must continually monitor and refine the work they do to foster students' social and emotional development based on the growth achieved and the more stubborn challenges that emerge.

Let's take a closer look at each step in mounting an effective schoolwide SEL effort.

Use Data to Guide Decision Making

Begin where you are by examining your school's current status. Some of this work is obvious, such as analyzing student climate data to uncover places of strength and opportunities for growth. Most districts collect such data annually as part of safe and healthy schools initiatives, and they are a rich source of information about bullying, student-teacher relationships, and the learning milieu. These data should be further aggregated to analyze for trends by age; gender; and socioeconomic, language, and program status.

However, we advocate a "looking in the corners" approach to data analysis that seeks to move beyond the surface level to uncover facets of the data that are hiding in plain sight (James-Ward, Fisher, Frey, & Lapp, 2013, p. 38). As one example of looking in the corners, schools around the country have augmented their climate data with "student hot-spot maps." As part of the climate survey students complete, they receive a map of the school and are asked to circle areas where they feel less safe and where bullying occurs—these are often public spaces, such as the cafeteria and the bus boarding zone. These maps can alert adults to where their presence may be needed in the school and where they will have opportunities to reinforce SEL principles. The maps can also kick off conversations about whether the adults who are already in those spaces (e.g., cafeteria workers and supervisory personnel) have the necessary professional training and support to take effective action themselves.

A second vital source of data is the staff themselves. A portion of the Building Equity Audit is devoted to SEL (Smith et al., 2017). This auditing tool, developed and piloted at the school where we work, is used to survey staff and students on five facets of equity-driven schooling:

- Physical integration
- Social-emotional engagement
- Opportunity to learn
- Instructional excellence
- Engaged and inspired learners

The 20 questions on the social-emotional engagement section of the audit are designed to probe beliefs about the effectiveness of the school's systems for supporting student's counseling and mental health needs, as well as discipline and attendance policies (see Figure 7.1).

FIGURE 7.1

Assessment of Social-Emotional Engagement Within Your School

SOCIAL-EMOTIONAL ENGAGEMENT

1. The social and emotional needs of students—from prosocial skills to responsiveness to trauma—are adequately supported in our school.
2. Students feel safe at school.
3. Teachers know what to do if a student's mental health and well-being are in question.
4. Students who need counseling and social services receive them.
5. Bullying is not a problem at our school.
6. There are students who are afraid to come to school.
7. Teachers and staff show they care about students.
8. We care for, support, and mentor some students beyond their classroom performance.
9. Students have at least one adult in school who cares about, supports, and mentors them.
10. We promote positive race and human relations to better understand and interact with students from different backgrounds.
11. We are a culturally competent staff.
12. Our school has programs and policies that are designed to improve attendance.
13. We need to spend more time trying to improve attendance.
14. Our school's discipline plans are restorative rather than punitive.
15. Staff receive professional development to help us understand and implement our schoolwide discipline plan.
16. We understand and support our schoolwide approach to discipline.
17. Students value their relationships with teachers.
18. Students are treated equitably when they misbehave, and consequences are based on an ethic of care rather than demographic characteristics.
19. Students from specific subgroups are treated differently than others when they misbehave.
20. Students from specific subgroups are more likely to be sent out of class, suspended, or expelled.

Source: Reprinted from *Building Equity: Policies and Practices to Empower All Learners* (p. 193), by D. Smith, N. Frey, I. Pumpian, and D. Fisher, 2017, Alexandria, VA: ASCD. Copyright 2017 by ASCD.

Rather than addressing whether SEL principles are taught, we chose to focus on outcomes. Students who are fearful of school or who feel disconnected from it contribute to chronic absenteeism. Children whose relationships with peers and adults are fraught with tension spend more time out of class. Teachers are often acutely aware of the unmet needs of their students who bring more challenging mental health needs to school. Additional data sources that need to be examined through an SEL lens include attendance records and suspension and expulsion rates. Inequities related to these issues can reveal gaps and spotlight students who are in need of more intensive interventions.

A third data source is parents and families. We especially like getting the perspective of families who are new to the school where we work, as they haven't yet grown accustomed to the status quo. We send home a welcome letter and the first part of a family survey a few weeks after they have enrolled to gauge the effectiveness of our initial outreach (see Figure 7.2). The letter itself, we believe, sends a positive message to families about their value to the school organization. In addition, we send out the second part of the survey annually to all families to help identify areas for improvement. The information gathered from these tools builds a communication bridge between families and teachers.

Taken together, these data sources provide an initial view of the status of SEL in the school. These data should be shared with faculty as a means to open the discussion about SEL. Be mindful, though, that some members of your staff might want to rush straight to solutions, bypassing thoughtful analysis. This is a common error, and it tends to lead to bloated initiatives with too diffuse a focus and too many strategies that are difficult to monitor and support.

We use a simple protocol to foster analysis and questions before leaping to solutions. After sharing the data, we move into small groups of eight and follow a two-round process dubbed "Observe and Wonder." In the first round, each member spends five minutes writing objective observations, one per sticky note. Members share one observation at a time until all the observations have been shared. The group's facilitator then clusters the sticky notes together to capture similar observations and labels each cluster. In the second round, the process is repeated, this time using "I wonder . . ." as a question stem. After all the wonderings are shared, the facilitator (again with input

FIGURE 7.2

New Family Survey

We would like to know your opinions on how well our school is meeting your family's and child(ren)'s needs and how you feel about your school experience.

- There are no right or wrong answers. We are interested only in your opinions.
- Your answers will be kept private. Your answers will be combined with those of other parents in a report of the survey findings.
- Your input is very important. Findings of the survey will be summarized and used to improve the school's efforts in strengthening the partnership between parents and the school.

What is/are your child(ren)'s grade level(s)? (circle all that apply)

K   1   2   3   4   5   6   7   8   9   10   11   12

Were any of these children enrolled at our school last year?   ☐ Yes   ☐ No

When you visit the school...	ALL of the time	MOST of the time	SOME of the time	NONE of the time
Is the reception staff friendly and helpful?				
Are the teachers easy to talk to?				
Are the administrators easy to talk to?				
Do you feel welcomed?				

What is/are the best way(s) to communicate with you and/or your family? (choose all that apply)

☐ School memos (e-mails, website, letters, etc.)
☐ Children's teachers
☐ Counselor
☐ Direct contact (phone call, school/home visit, meeting)
☐ Other (please specify): _____

What else would you like to tell us about communication at our school?_____

_____

_____

_____

continued

FIGURE 7.2 (continued)
New Family Survey

Last school year, were you contacted by someone from the school regarding… (choose all that apply)

☐ Your child's academic success

☐ Your child's academic struggles

☐ Your child's positive social behavior

☐ Your child's negative social behavior

☐ Your child's recognition in achievement (sports, music, volunteerism, etc.)

☐ No reason, just to make contact (say hello, introduce self, etc.)

☐ Other (please specify): _____

What else would you like to tell us about contact regarding your child's successes and difficulties?

_____

_____

How much do you agree or disagree with the following statements?	STRONGLY agree	AGREE	DISAGREE	STRONGLY disagree
The school has high expectations for my child.				
The school clearly communicates those expectations to me and my child(ren).				
My child is learning what he or she needs to know to be successful after graduating.				
My child receives assistance when he or she is having difficulty academically or socially.				
The curriculum and activities keep my child interested and motivated.				
My child is happy at school.				

What else would you like to tell us about our school?_____

_____

_____

Thank you for taking the time to complete this survey. We can't be the Best School in the Universe without families like yours.

from the group) clusters questions—and now identifies categories. The large group comes together, and each group shares the categories they distilled from their data analysis. The categories speak to the patterns within and across data sources without getting bogged down in individual strategies that can derail the process. The discussion concludes after the group generates a list of the key stakeholders that need to be involved, based on initial findings, and what further insights the organization hopes to gain from these individuals.

Include Key Stakeholders

The success of an SEL initiative increases exponentially with the involvement of families, students, and school staff, including classified and certificated personnel. When you consider that every moment of a child's day (and an adult's, for that matter) is touched by social and emotional skills and dispositions, it makes sense to enlist a broad range of stakeholders, all of whom can provide impressions and ideas about current needs and strengths of the student body, and organizational policies that inhibit or enhance SEL. Student focus groups are an excellent source and should be formed with diverse experiences in mind. After all, elected leaders on student governance are likely to have a different perspective than students who do not belong to any school club or participate in any school sports. Again, you want to look into the corners, gathering as many perspectives as you can.

These student groups should be led by a moderator who can keep the conversation going and make sure it stays focused on a modest list of prepared questions (5–10 at most). Telling the members of the focus group about the purpose of the exercise also enlists them in the initiative. We have found it useful to share some pertinent data with the focus group and ask them for their reactions ("Are you surprised by the data on student beliefs about caring? Is it higher or lower than you thought?"). Next, we ask them about their vision of a positive alternative. For instance, you might share data with the cafeteria staff about the number of times this location was cited as a hot spot, garnering their reactions to the data, followed by asking for a description of what a more peaceable cafeteria would look like. At the school where we work, we post survey data on the flat screen in our front office along with the prompt, "How might we do better?" to solicit ideas. Some of the data have been previously identified as problematic indicators. We ask viewers for reactions they can write anonymously and place in a nearby suggestion box. We have been pleasantly surprised by the level of participation, especially from extended family members who are at the school to pick up a child or attend a meeting. Keep the public relations aspect of these approaches in mind. By virtue of asking, you are inviting stakeholders into the decision-making process and signaling your values.

Identify Needs and Goals

To determine your school's specific needs and goals, we suggest using root cause analysis: examining the data-demonstrated and stakeholder-informed needs, considering the internal and external factors that might be hampering student progress, and figuring out what you will do to tear those barriers down (or provide routes over or around them). A veteran district administrator once said to us, "Each system is exquisitely tuned to produce the results it gets." This is true, so why not explore how changing the system might change those results?

The root cause analysis protocol we use incorporates six factors (James-Ward et al., 2013):

- *Student factors.* Many student factors beyond demographics data can be enlightening, including attendance and student climate data (e.g., impressions of school).
- *External factors.* Although outside the school, these factors (e.g., fiscal support, community crime rates, access to libraries, parent support) can influence what happens inside the school.
- *Organizational structure.* Every school has a structure that includes personnel, roles and responsibilities, and internal accountability procedures. For instance, does the school use professional learning communities or some other collaborative process? Does the school counselor or social worker have opportunities to meet with these teams to discuss data?
- *Organizational culture.* The interactions that occur within a school can inhibit or enhance the organizational culture. A school whose entire

student body meets outside each morning to begin the day has a different organizational culture than one who gathers together only a few times a year for assemblies. A school that requires "learning walks" by grade level or department for the purpose of teacher collaboration has a different organizational culture than one whose unspoken expectation is that people don't observe one another in the act of teaching.

- *Instruction.* We purposely locate these last two factors—instruction and curriculum—until later in the root cause analysis process precisely because they are often the ones schools gravitate to first to fix a problem. Quality instruction is a chief indicator of what happens, or does not happen, in schools. But moving immediately to this factor without first considering the other systems that can inhibit quality instruction can be tantamount to rearranging deck chairs on a sinking ship.
- *Curriculum.* When it comes to SEL, many schools respond by purchasing a program and then calling it a day. To be sure, there are a number of reliable free and commercial programs available. But there are also lots of highly rated car models available for purchase; just because it is a good vehicle doesn't mean it is the right one for you. Similarly, the selection of a program or approach should come only after careful study of what your school needs.

Some of the factors identified through the root cause analysis will be impossible to address through school efforts. However, that doesn't mean they shouldn't be named. And it is crucial to add that, although these factors exist, they don't necessarily predict student outcomes. For example, the Consortium of Chicago Schools Research (Bryk, Sebring, Allensworth, Luppescu, & Easton, 2010; Burdick-Will, 2013) reports that the best predictors of school safety are the social capital within the organization, the academic achievement of its students, and students' relationships with adults. Student poverty and the community crime rate were *not* predictors of school safety. In other words, investing in SEL to promote a positive network of students and adults works to promote achievement and safe spaces, even though it does not change the students' socioeconomic status or the community crime rate.

Once root causes have surfaced, the work group can move to developing goals that will steer monitoring and evaluation methods. A common form of goal development is the SMART goal process. SMART goals are specific, measurable, attainable, results-oriented, and time-bound. These are really a series of goals, not just one, and should be used to gauge progress and effectiveness. For example, SMART goals related to an SEL initiative might read like this:

- By the end of the school year, students in grades K–1 will be able to provide at least three examples of how they manage their emotions when feeling sad, worried, or afraid. (Emotional Regulation)
- By the end of the first quarter, middle school students will be able to identify techniques they use to study for tests and reflect on how well they used those techniques. (Cognitive Regulation)
- By the end of 9th grade, all students will have proposed, implemented, and reflected on a service learning project. (Public Spirit)

Goals that have been developed using data from a variety of sources and stakeholders are goals that are more likely to be achieved. A root cause analysis further informs the goals used by a school because it takes into consideration the many factors that have contributed to the current state of the school. This is crucial for developing a viable SEL learning initiative, because it avoids the naïve thinking trap that we just need to "fix" students and then everything will be fine. By carefully examining systems and developing goals that align to needs, we equip ourselves with the ability to monitor progress and evaluate programs.

Select a Program or Approach Based on Goals

Clearly it would be a big mistake to buy into an SEL program or approach without carefully considering the data, involving stakeholders, and identifying site-specific needs and goals. Without data analysis, a school risks blindly selecting a program with little evidence of need. A failure to involve stakeholders virtually guarantees that an initiative will be doomed by limited buy-in by teachers, students, or families. Instead, it will be perceived as one more thing to do, and it's almost certain to be the first practice dropped when the schedule gets too crowded. Even a carefully researched program or approach risks an implementation dip without goals that have been aligned to identified needs. SMART goals provide school leaders and the teaching staff with ways to monitor and adjust practices.

Now, equipped with all of this information, it is time to select a program or approach. It is quite possible that the identified needs of the school are such that a locally designed approach is what will work best. Many districts choose this path because they want to customize their efforts based on community-based cultural norms, local strengths, and opportunities to partner with external agencies. If your school or district decides that a customized approach is the correct path, keep these quality indicators in mind for developing an effective system (Jones et al., 2017):

- *Classroom activities should include, and extend beyond, core lessons.* SEL principles must be integrated into academic subjects and disciplines, as well as nonacademic settings such as lunch, recess, afterschool programs, sports, and clubs.
- *Schoolwide efforts to improve culture and climate should actively support in-class efforts.* Morning routines, front office procedures, and website and social media channels should be used to promote SEL efforts.
- *After-school programs should be leveraged to support SEL efforts.* Program development should include materials and strategies for afterschool personnel to utilize. This is especially important in cases where these personnel are not official members of the school staff.
- *SEL approaches should capitalize on the local context.* Don't overlook long-standing community partners such as universities and businesses to amplify SEL efforts. Involve the parent-teacher organization in the ongoing implementation of the program.
- *Schedule ongoing professional learning opportunities to deepen the skills of adults.* Too many initiatives fail because the PD failed to go beyond the initial introduction to an effort. And don't forget those who join the organization after the SEL initiative has been underway for a while. How do people new to the school learn about this program?

- *Designate support for the SEL effort.* As noted earlier, follow-up and coaching are required to move from initial adoption to sustained efforts. However, these don't simply happen. School leaders should work with faculty to devise ways to provide ongoing support of teachers.
- *Use tools aligned to goals to assess outcomes.* These can include checklists and other informal tools for teachers to use to assess student performance, as well as surveys to gather reflections of the adults involved in this effort. SMART goals provide a means for determining student outcomes and identifying necessary refinements.
- *Use tools to assess implementation.* New initiatives can be slow to start or may enjoy an early burst of energy, followed by a drifting away from the mission as the school year progresses. Implementation tools such as logs and classroom walkthroughs can be used to assess the level of schoolwide implementation that is occurring.
- *Maximize family engagement efforts.* Families are among the very best resources we have, yet schools sometimes fail to maximize what they can accomplish. Families cannot support school-based SEL efforts if they don't know what is happening. Be sure to include information in family letters or school newsletters, and schedule informational events at school that focus on SEL and the link to academics.
- *Engage the community.* A true expression of the outcomes of SEL efforts is in the ways young people serve their communities. Schools can cultivate community partners to support service learning projects. As well, community leaders should be invited to share their expertise at career fairs, family nights, and other events.

These same principles apply to commercial SEL curriculum programs and should be features to look for when assessing their relative fit for your school or district. We can't say enough about the usefulness of the tool developed through sponsorship from the Wallace Foundation called *Navigating SEL from the Inside Out* (Jones et al., 2017). The researchers examined 25 elementary SEL programs and provide detailed information for each, enabling comparison. The report includes specific information about the quality indicators presented here, as well as guidance for selection and implementation.

The Whole Child Approach

ASCD's Whole Child approach (www.ascd.org/whole-child.aspx) is another powerful tool for SEL-focused schools. The five tenets of the Whole Child approach speak directly to the intentions outlined in this book:

1. Each student enters school **healthy** and learns about and practices a healthy lifestyle.
2. Each student learns in an environment that is physically and emotionally **safe** for students and adults.
3. Each student is actively **engaged** in learning and is connected to the school and broader community.
4. Each student has access to personalized learning and is **supported** by qualified, caring adults.
5. Each student is **challenged** academically and prepared for success in college or further study and for employment and participation in a global environment.

The ASCD School Improvement Tool (http://sitool.ascd.org/) is a needs assessment survey aligned with these tenets. It collects data for schools as they apply to school climate and culture, family and community engagement, professional development, and staff capacity. The School Improvement Tool can provide your school or district with valuable information about your current status as it applies to social and emotional learning.

Takeaways

We began Chapter 1 with an argument for why it is time for social and emotional learning to receive more attention. As we have emphasized, the truth is that educators are engaged in SEL whether they intend to be or not. The way we teach, how we teach, and what we choose *not* to teach and *not* to do communicate our values loud and clear. In a time when the world seems to be moving at ever-increasing speed, young people look to the adults around them for wisdom about how to be an engaged and inspired person—to help them the develop the essential skills they need for the classroom and beyond.

In fact, some us of may be wondering what took educators so long to fully embrace this responsibility. It's been said, "The best time to have planted a tree was 20 years ago. The second best time to plant a tree is today."

What tree will you plant? And when?

Appendix: Literary Resources for Social and Emotional Learning

Narrative and informational texts are an excellent way to spark conversations about tenets of social and emotional learning. Many examples are referenced throughout the book, although they are by no means exhaustive. Helen Foster James, literacy researcher and children's book author, has assembled this annotated list to provide even more examples of titles to consider when integrating SEL with your instruction.

Resources for Teaching Identity and Agency (Chapter 2)

PICTURE BOOKS

Brennan-Nelson, D., & Brennan, R. (2008). *Willow*. Ann Arbor, MI: Sleeping Bear Press. Willow has an artistic spirit and expression, and she doesn't always follow rules in art class. Though reprimanded, she doesn't lose her confidence.

Byrd, B. (1994). *The table where rich people sit*. New York: Atheneum. Mountain Girl resents that her parents don't care more about money and having fancy things, but her family sits around a table and discusses what "rich" really is and how it is seen in a person's life.

Carlson, N. (1988). *I like me!* New York: Viking Press. This book's star is a peppy pig with positive feelings about herself and lots of confidence. When she makes a mistake, she picks herself up and tries again.

Caseley, J. (2001). *Bully.* New York: HarperCollins/Greenwillow. When Mickey's best friend, Jack, turns into a bully, Mickey's mother and father offer advice on how to handle the situation. Mickey learns that Jack feels displaced by his new baby sister and is angry and hurt.

Choi, Y. (2008). *The name jar.* New York: Dragonfly Books. Unhei has just moved from Korea and is the new kid at school. She is anxious about telling them her hard-to-pronounce name and decides she'll tell them next week when she picks her name from a glass jar.

DeMont, B. (2017). *I love my purse.* Toronto: Annick Press. Charlie loves his bright red purse his grandmother let him have, but others have a problem with it. Even the crossing guard asks him about his "strange" choice.

Dr. Seuss. (1996). *My many colored days.* New York: Random House. Using a spectrum of vibrant colors and a menagerie of animals, the book showcases a range of emotions and prompts discussions of emotions with children.

Engle, M. (2015). *Drum dream girl: How one girl's courage changed music.* Boston: Houghton Mifflin Harcourt. Long ago on an island there was a rule that girls could not be drummers, until drum dream girl decided to play bongos and practiced in secret. Based on the childhood of Millo Castro Zaldarriaga, a Chinese-African-Cuban girl. (Nonfiction)

Henkes, K. (1991). *Chrysanthemum.* New York: HarperCollins/Greenwillow. Chrysanthemum, a mouse, starts kindergarten and is teased by her classmates because of her name. She loses and then regains her confidence.

Leaf, M. (1936). *The story of Ferdinand.* New York: Viking Press. Ferdinand isn't like all the other bulls. He is content to just sit and smell the flowers while others snort, leap, and butt their heads.

Lovell, P. (2001). *Stand tall, Molly Lou Melon.* **New York: Putnam.** Molly Melon is short, is clumsy, has buck teeth, and has an unusual voice, but she doesn't mind. Her grandmother told her to walk proud, and she takes her grandma's advice.

Parr, T. (2001). *It's okay to be different.* **New York: Little, Brown.** Through bright, childlike illustrations and text, Parr says that it's OK to be different from others, an important first step in getting children to accept one another.

Saltzberg, B. (2010). *Beautiful oops!* **New York: Workman Publishing.** Clumsy kids will especially appreciate this imaginative book, which shows how mistakes can turn an oops into something wonderful.

Uegaki, C. (2005). *Suki's kimono.* **Boston: Kids Can Press.** Suki's favorite possession is her blue cotton kimono, a gift from her grandmother. She's determined to wear it on the first day of school. Suki marches to her own drumbeat.

Viorst, J. (1987). *The tenth good thing about Barney.* **New York: Atheneum.** A boy's cat dies. His mother suggests they have a funeral and that he think of 10 good things about Barney to share at the funeral. This is a classic story of dealing with a pet's death.

Wood, A. (1982). *Quick as a cricket.* **Auburn, ME: Child's Play.** This favorite story spotlights how the many qualities of one child, compared to many animals, come together to represent the child as a whole.

CHAPTER BOOKS

Abdel-Fattah, R. (2014). *Does my head look big in this?* **New York: Scholastic.** High school junior Amal decides to begin wearing the hijab and experiences racist taunts, troubles with boys, and academic worries. At turns funny and poignant, this book provides lots of opportunity to talk about identity.

Crutcher, C. (1995). *Ironman.* **New York: HarperCollins.** When 17-year-old Bo attends an anger management group at school, he begins to examine his relationship with his father, who bullies him.

George, J. C. (1959). *My side of the mountain.* **New York: Dutton.** This classic novel features a boy who learns about courage, independence, and the need for companionship while attempting to live in a forested area of New York state. A Newbery Honor Book.

Hinton, S. E. (1967). *The outsiders.* **New York: Viking Press.** This is a classic novel about a boy on the outskirts of society who can rely on only his brothers and his band of friends.

Lin, G. (2006). *The Year of the Dog.* **New York: Little, Brown.** It's the Chinese Year of the Dog—the year Pacy is supposed to "find herself"—but that's hard to do when you are trying to fit in at school and please your immigrant parents. Universal themes of friendship, family, and finding one's passion in life make this novel appealing.

Lindgren, A. (1945). *Pippi Longstocking.* **New York: Penguin.** Pippi is unconventional but full of confidence. Adults find her exasperating at times. She enjoys telling tall tales of her memories of sailing across the world.

Mead, A. (1998). *Junebug and the reverend.* **New York: Farrar.** In this sequel to Mead's book *Junebug,* the protagonist's life is changing for the better as his family leaves the projects and makes a new start. His sister, Tasha, makes friends easily, but Junebug becomes the target of bullying. An effective portrayal of a resilient child in a difficult situation.

O'Dell, S. (1960). *Island of the blue dolphins.* **Boston: Houghton Mifflin.** This story of a 12-year-old girl stranded alone for years on an island is loosely based on a true story of a Nicoleño Native American girl who was left alone during the 19th century. A story of strength and the ability to handle life while being alone. A Newbery Medal book.

Park, B. (1995). *Mick Harte was here.* **New York: Random House.** Phoebe tells the story of her younger brother, Mick, who dies in a bicycle accident, and her struggle to deal with his death and her own grief.

Paulsen, G. (1987). *Hatchet.* **New York: Atheneum.** The ultimate survival classic tells how 13-year-old Brian is left alone for 54 days and how he makes mistakes and is triumphant. A Newbery Honor book.

Spinelli, J. (2000). *Stargirl.* **New York: Scholastic.** Stargirl has a unique personality and comes to school in strange outfits. The most popular girl at school declares that Stargirl is a fake, but Leo thinks Stargirl is kind and brave. The two start a friendship, but then Leo tries to convince Stargirl to act more "normal."

Wiesel, E. (1972). *Night.* **New York: Hill and Wang.** This is a classic first-person account of Wiesel's harrowing survival of the Holocaust and his search to find meaning and forgiveness for himself while questioning how God could have let such horror occur. (Nonfiction)

Resources for Teaching Emotional Regulation (Chapter 3)

PICTURE BOOKS

Bang, M. (1999). *When Sophie gets angry—Really, really angry.* **New York: Scholastic.** Everybody gets angry sometimes, and it can be very upsetting. What does Sophie do when she gets angry, and what do you do? A Caldecott Honor book.

Bottner, B. (1992). *Bootsie Barker bites.* **New York: Putnam.** While her mother visits with Bootsie's mother, the narrator is subjected to Bootsie's unpleasant games, which frequently involve biting. Faced with the prospect of having Bootsie spend the night, the narrator turns the tables on Bootsie by inventing a new game to play.

Brimner, L. D. (1998). *Elliot Fry's good-bye.* **Honesdale, PA: Boyds Mills Press.** When Elliot's mom scolds him for tracking mud into the house, frustrated Elliot decides to pack his suitcase and leave home.

Carlson, N. (1994). *How to lose all your friends.* **New York: Viking.** With humor, Carlson pokes fun at bullies and others who have a hard time attracting and keeping friends. This tongue-in-cheek book invites discussion about what characteristics true friends exhibit.

Dewdney, A. (2007). *Llama Llama mad at mama.* **New York: Scholastic.** Little Llama Llama is bored, loses his patience, and throws a tantrum while shopping at the store, but Mama Llama keeps her cool and involves him in the shopping chore. He learns that being with Mama is what's important. Llama Llama's poor behavior will spark discussion.

Henkes, K. (1996). *Lilly's purple plastic purse.* **New York: HarperCollins.** Lilly brings her purse to school and can't wait until sharing time, but her teacher confiscates her treasures, which leads to Lilly's anger, revenge, remorse, and then her efforts to make amends.

Henkes, K. (2000). *Wemberly worried.* **New York: HarperCollins.** Wemberly worries about everything—big, little, and in between. It's time for school to start, and now he's worrying even more.

Krull, K., & Brewer, P. (2010). *Lincoln tells a joke: How laughter saved the president (and the country).* **Boston: Houghton Mifflin Harcourt.** This story presents a positive portrait that humanizes this favorite president and shows how his love of laughter was what kept him going even in difficult times. (Nonfiction)

Manning, J. (2012). *Millie fierce.* **New York: Penguin.** Millie is quiet and sweet but gets ignored, so she decides she wants to be fierce. She soon realizes being fierce isn't working either, so she adds some kindness to the mix.

Naylor, P. R. (1994). *The king of the playground.* **New York: Aladdin.** Each day Sammy threatens Kevin, proclaiming himself "King of the Playground." Kevin and his father discuss Sammy's actions, and Kevin gains the confidence to resolve the conflict.

O'Neill, A. (2002). *The recess queen.* New York: Scholastic. In this rollicking, rhyming story about the power of kindness and friendship, a schoolyard bully is enlightened by the new kid in class.

Polacco, P. (2001). *Mr. Lincoln's way.* New York: Philomel. The principal, Mr. Lincoln, tries to help Eugene (aka "Mean Green Fighting Gene") change his behavior by giving him a book about birds and letting him create a bird atrium at the school, but Gene continues to make racist comments.

Sendak, M. (1963). *Where the Wild Things are.* New York: Harper. Max wreaks havoc in his household and is sent to bed without supper. His bedroom undergoes a mysterious transformation, and he becomes king of the Wild Things in this classic picture book. A Caldecott Medal book.

Shannon, D. (1998). *No, David!* New York: Blue Sky Press. When David Shannon was 5 years old, he wrote a semi-autobiographical story of a little boy who broke all his mother's rules and all he could hear was his mother's voice saying, "No, David!" A Caldecott Honor book.

Vail, R., & Heo, Y. (2002). *Sometimes I'm Bombaloo.* New York: Scholastic. Sometimes Katie loses her temper and uses her feet and fists instead of words. She's mad and just not herself. She calls herself "Bombaloo." A little time-out and some understanding can help Katie feel like Katie again.

Viorst, J. (1972). *Alexander and the terrible, horrible, no good, very bad day.* New York: Atheneum. From the moment Alexander wakes up, his day is going the wrong way. He says he thinks he wants to move to Australia where he's certain things will be better.

Willems, M. (2012). *My friend is sad.* New York: Walker & Company. Gerald is down in the dumps, and his friend Piggie is determined to cheer him up by dressing as a cowboy, a clown, and even a robot, but what does it take to make a sad elephant happy?

Wood, A. (1996). *Elbert's bad word.* Boston: Houghton Mifflin Harcourt. Elbert overhears an ugly word and decides to use it when he's upset, but learns there are other words that are better choices for letting off some steam.

CHAPTER BOOKS

Aurelius, M. (2017). *Mediations.* **New York: CreateSpace.** Written in 180 CE, this is a document of Roman emperor Marcus Aurelius's intellectual journey and search for self-improvement while planning a series of military campaigns. (Nonfiction)

Birney, B. G. (2005). *The seven wonders of Sassafras Springs.* **New York: Atheneum.** Life in Sassafras Springs has always been predictable, even boring, but one day Eben McAllister's pa challenges him to find seven wonders in Sassafras Springs that can rival the real Seven Wonders of the World.

Bruel, N. (2012). *Bad Kitty: School daze.* **New York: Square Fish.** When Kitty misbehaves, she is sent to obedience school where she must learn to like others and listen and follow rules.

DiCamillo, K. (2000). *Because of Winn-Dixie.* **Sommerville, MA: Candlewick Press.** The importance and power of friendship is prevalent throughout this Newbery Honor novel as 10-year-old Opal Buloni moves to a new town to live with her father. She likes stories and asks her father to tell her 10 things about her mother, who left her when she was young.

Hall, M. K., & Jones, K. (Eds.) (2011). *Dear bully: Seventy authors tell their stories.* **New York: HarperCollins.** Favorite authors for teens and young people share their stories about bullying, as bystanders, victims, or the bully. There are 70 heartfelt and empathetic stories from each corner of the schoolyard. The book is a resource for teens, educators, and parents, and it includes suggestions for further reading. (Nonfiction)

Hillenbrand, L. (2014). *Unbroken: A World War II story of survival, resilience, and redemption.* **New York: Random House.** Louis Zamperini competes in the 1936 Olympics in front of Hitler, joins the military, and then survives a plane crash and 47 days on a raft in the Pacific. And that's just the beginning of his remarkable story. (Nonfiction)

McDonald, M. (2000). *Judy Moody was in a mood.* **New York: Scholastic.** Judy Moody doesn't have high hopes for 3rd grade. Any kid who has ever been in a bad mood will be able to identify with this feisty, funny, and ever-changing character.

O'Connor, B. (2009). *The small adventure of Popeye and Elvis.* **New York: Farrar/Francis Foster Books.** Nothing ever happens in Fayette, South Carolina—or at least that's what Popeye thinks. His whole life has been boring, boring, boring, but things start to look up when a Rambler gets stuck in the mud, trapping Elvis and his five rowdy siblings in town.

Palacio, R. J. (2012). *Wonder.* **New York: Knopf.** August Pullman has been homeschooled, but his parents think it's time for him to experience a larger world and attend school. Auggie, who was born with a severe facial difference, must navigate his new school, make friends, and grow in personal strength. He is a hero who illustrates that you can't blend in when you were born to be different.

Park, B. (2001). *Junie B. Jones first grader (at last!).* **New York: Random House.** Junie is starting 1st grade with a new classroom, new students, and a new teacher, and she soon learns she might need glasses.

Paterson, K. (1978). *Bridge to Terabithia.* **New York: Harper Row.** Fifth grader Jesse Aarons makes friends with Leslie, a smart, talented, outgoing tomboy from a wealthier family. Together they invent a land called Terabithia. A Newbery Medal book.

Telgemeier, R. (2010). *Smile.* **New York: Scholastic/Graphix.** Raina trips and smashes her two front teeth. Sixth grade is hard enough without having to endure dental treatments. Based on the author's life, this graphic novel encourages kids to believe they can get through troubled times.

Resources for Teaching Cognitive Regulation (Chapter 4)

PICTURE BOOKS

Bunting, E. (1993). *Fly away home.* **Boston: Houghton Mifflin Harcourt.** A homeless boy who lives in an airport, moving from terminal to terminal to avoid being noticed, is inspired by a trapped bird's search for freedom.

Cronin, D. (2000). *Click, clack, moo: Cows that type.* **New York: Simon & Schuster.** Farmer Brown's cows have a typewriter and are requesting changes from the farmer or they'll go on strike.

DiSalvo, D. (2002). *Spaghetti Park.* **New York: Holiday House.** In this story of community spirit, Angelo organizes the restoration of a seedy neighborhood park that is a hangout for "troublemakers." Centering the action on the park's bocce court, DiSalvo shows the tough kids looking on with increasing interest while local residents work to rejuvenate the park. A page of bocce ball rules is included.

DiSalvo-Ryan, D. (1994). *City green.* **New York: HarperCollins.** Marcy is motivated to act when the city condemns and demolishes a building in her neighborhood. Soon everyone is donating time and energy. Instructions for starting a community garden are included.

Fleming, C. (2003). *Boxes for Katje.* **New York: Farrar/Melanie Kroupa.** After World War II, Rosie, an American girl, sends a goodwill package to Katje, a girl in Holland. Katje, in turn, is inspired to share the gifts she receives with others in her Dutch town. Based on an experience from the author's mother's childhood.

Galdone, P. (1973). *The little red hen.* **Boston: Houghton Mifflin Harcourt.** The little red hen plants some seeds, but who will help her harvest the crop? There are various versions of this popular folktale, and the story always prompts discussions about working together.

Judge, L. (2007). *One thousand tracings: Healing the wounds of World War II*. New York: Hyperion. Based on her family's history, Judge's book tells how her grandparents organized a relief effort from their Midwest farm and sent care packages to more than 3,000 desperate people in Europe.

Krull, K. (1996). *Wilma unlimited*. San Diego, CA: Harcourt Brace. A fascinating biography of Olympian Wilma Rudolph, who overcame overwhelming adversities of poverty, racial discrimination, and polio to become an American hero. (Nonfiction)

Lobel, A. (1972). *Frog and Toad together*. New York: Harper & Row. In one of the stories from this book, "This List," Toad wakes up one morning and decides to make a list of things he must do today.

McPhail, D. (2002). *The teddy bear*. New York: Holt. When a young boy spots his lost bear in the park and realizes a homeless man has adopted it, he demonstrates his compassion by sharing his beloved teddy with the man.

Muth, J. J. (2003). *Stone soup*. New York: Scholastic. Strangers with very little work as a team when one stranger suggests making soup with a stone. The result is a feast, demonstrating the power of cooperation. There are numerous versions of this classic tale.

Newman, P. (2018). *Neema's reason to smile*. New York: Lightswitch Learning. Neema wants to go to school. Her family can't afford it, but she's determined to make her dreams happen. An important story with themes of equal access to education, global education, and achieving goals.

Polacco, P. (1998). *Thank you, Mr. Falker*. New York: Philomel. Trisha endures the cruel taunts of classmates who call her "dumb" and falls behind in her studies, but her new 5th grade teacher, Mr. Falker, helps her develop her talents. Students who struggle with learning difficulties will find reassurance in Trisha's success, and classmates may empathize with her struggles.

Woodson, J. (2012). *Each kindness*. New York: Penguin. Chloe and her friends won't play with Maya, the new girl, but her teacher demonstrates how small acts of kindness can change the world, and Chloe thinks about how she should have treated Maya. Winner of the Jane Addams Peace Award.

Wyeth, S. D. (1998). *Something beautiful*. New York: Doubleday. A little girl searches for "something beautiful" in her inner-city neighborhood and manages to find beauty in many places. She then identifies a way she can contribute to the beauty surrounding her.

CHAPTER BOOKS

Buyea, R. (2017). *The perfect score*. New York: Delacorte. Sixth graders work on a community service project while also figuring out ways to prepare for and pass the annual assessment test. They learn how to overcome their personal flaws to form a better whole. Topics of sibling abuse, poverty, learning disabilities, and competitive sports are showcased.

Clements, A. (1996). *Frindle*. New York: Scholastic. Nick Allen learns how words are created and decides to get his friends to use his created word for pen, "frindle." Soon people in his town are using the word *frindle*. Then the word becomes used around the country, and Nick becomes a local hero.

Covey, S. (2014). *The 7 habits of highly effective teens*. New York: Touchstone. A guide for success, as reinterpreted for adolescents. (Nonfiction)

Curtis, C. P. (1999). *Bud, not Buddy*. New York: Delacorte Books. Ten-year-old Bud Caldwell has just been placed in his third foster family, four years after his mother's death. He is determined to find his father. A Newbery Medal book.

Ellis, D. (2017). *Sit*. Toronto: Groundwood Books. A collection of stories from different countries, each featuring a child who makes a decision and takes action. Every protagonist shares the common goal of survival, and the novel will spark discussion about choice and social injustice.

Ignatow, A. (2010). *The popularity papers: Research for the social improvement and general betterment of Lydia Goldblatt and Julie Graham-Chang.* New York: Amulet. Two 5th grade friends, Lydia and Julie, are determined to uncover the secrets of popularity. They record, discuss, and replicate behaviors of "cool" girls. This is the first of a seven-book series.

Lansing, A. (2005). *Endurance: Shackleton's incredible voyage.* New York: Basic Books. "Fortitudine vincimus" (By endurance we conquer) was Ernest Shackleton's family motto and a way of life. This is a document of his 1914 failed attempt to reach the South Pole and the remarkable achievement of saving all of his men once they are shipwrecked. (Nonfiction)

Lowry, L. (1993). *The giver.* Boston: Houghton Mifflin Harcourt. This haunting story centers on 12-year-old Jonas, who lives in a world of conformity and contentment, and raises questions about why our feelings and relationships matter. A Newbery Medal book.

Paulsen, G. (2011). *Flat broke: The theory, practice and destructive properties of greed.* New York: Random/Lamb. Kevin's allowance has been discontinued and he's desperate for money. He sees himself as a kingmaker and decides to create projects for others and take a cut of the profits. He's seeking money, fame, and fortune in the free enterprise system.

Pink, D. (2011). *Drive: The surprising truth about what motivates us.* New York: Riverhead. The author shares the latest in psychological research about how to best motivate ourselves and others. (Nonfiction)

Rocklin, J. (2012). *One day and one amazing morning on Orange Street.* New York: Abrams. When a mysterious man arrives on Orange Street, the block's children try to find out who he is and why he's there. The story of their orange tree connects each of them and their personal worries, from impressing friends to dealing with an expanding family to understanding a younger sibling's illness.

Ryan, P. M. (1998). *Riding freedom.* **New York: Scholastic.** This is a fictionalized story based on the life of Charlotte (Charley) Parkhurst, who ran away from an orphanage, posed as a boy, and moved to California, where she drove stagecoaches. A story of grit and determination.

Vawter, V. (2013). *Paperboy.* **New York: Dell.** Little Man is an awesome ball player but can't talk without stuttering. He's helping his best friend by doing his paper route for the month of July, and Little Man is not looking forward to talking with customers.

Resources for Teaching Social Skills (Chapter 5)

PICTURE BOOKS

Berger, S. (2018). *What if . . .* **New York: Little, Brown.** Creativity, the power of imagination, and the importance of self-expression are showcased in this picture book, written and illustrated by real-life best friends.

Brimner, L. D. (2002). *The sidewalk patrol.* **New York: Children's Press.** Abby and her friends call themselves the Corner Kids and help in their neighborhood by moving bicycles so their blind neighbor can walk safely on the sidewalk.

Chinn, K. (1995). *Sam and the lucky money.* **New York: Lee & Low.** Sam gets four dollars for Chinese New Year, but he is frustrated that it won't buy what he wants until he sees a homeless man and decides how he can best use his money.

de la Peña, M. (2015). *Last stop on Market Street.* **New York: Penguin.** Nana helps C.J. see the beauty in his surroundings as they take their bus to the soup kitchen every Sunday afternoon. Nana says, "Sometimes when you're surrounded by dirt, C.J., you're a better witness for what's beautiful." A Newbery Medal and Caldecott Honor book.

Golenbock, P. (1990). *Teammates*. Boston: Houghton Mifflin Harcourt. Jackie Robinson was the first black player on a Major League Baseball team, and this book describes how on one fateful day in Cincinnati, Pee Wee Reese took a stand and declared Jackie his teammate. (Nonfiction)

Ludwig, T. (2013). *The invisible boy*. New York: Penguin. Brian is a quiet boy and isn't noticed by his classmates until Justin joins his class. This story inspires children to think about how Brian might have felt and, perhaps, to act like Justin when they see someone who is excluded in a group.

Munson, D. (2010). *Enemy pie*. San Francisco: Chronicle. Summer is excellent until Jeremy moves into the neighborhood and becomes the enemy. Dad has a way of getting rid of enemies: give him an enemy pie. But the secret recipe includes spending an entire day playing with the enemy.

Palacio, R. J. (2017). *We're all wonders*. New York: Penguin. Auggie looks different from other children, but he hopes people will see past his looks and appreciate him. A powerful story of accepting others for who they are and not how they look.

Saltzberg, B. (2003). *Crazy hair day*. Somerville, MA: Candlewick. On school picture day, Stanley Birdbaum arrives at school thinking it's crazy hair day. After his friend Larry teases Stanley about his ridiculous do, Stanley hides in the bathroom. The teacher asks Larry "to be a peacemaker instead of a troublemaker," and Larry finally coaxes Stanley back to the class, where Stanley discovers everyone modeling sympathy dos for their group picture.

Thomas, S. M. (1998). *Somewhere today: A book of peace*. Park Ridge, IL: Albert Whitman. This book showcases examples of people promoting peace by doing various things to help and care for one another, such as teaching a younger child to ride a bike and choosing friendship over fighting. (Nonfiction)

Tolstoy, A. (2003). *The enormous turnip*. Boston: Houghton Mifflin Harcourt. A man plants a turnip and encourages it to grow, but it becomes too large for him to pull out on his own, and he gets others to help. This classic Russian folktale demonstrates the value of working together and the power of cooperation. Various versions of this tale are available.

CHAPTER BOOKS

Alexander, K. (2014). *The crossover*. Boston: Houghton Mifflin Harcourt. This story deals with coming to terms with a brother's new girlfriend, sibling rivalry, the pressure of playing basketball, and father-son relationships. Told in verse, this book won the Newbery Medal.

Clements, A. (2001). *Jake Drake: Bully buster*. New York: Atheneum. Jake questions, "So here's what I can't figure out. If everybody who works at school is so smart, how come they can't get rid of the bullies? How come when it comes to bullies, kids are mostly on their own?"

Cormier, R. (1974). *The chocolate war*. New York: Knopf. After refusing to sell chocolates in the annual fundraising drive, Jerry is bullied by his classmates and teacher in this young adult classic.

Estes, E. (1944). *The hundred dresses*. New York: Harcourt. Wanda Petronski is teased and taunted every day because she wears the same faded dress, but she says she has 100 beautiful dresses in many colors. She does—she's drawn them. A Newbery Honor book.

Frankl, V. (1959). *Man's search for meaning*. Boston: Beacon. Frankl recounts his experiences in four death camps during World War II and how his philosophical and spiritual interior life kept him alive. (Nonfiction)

Hahn, M. D. (1988). *December stillness*. New York: HarperCollins. Kelly finds herself at odds with her former friends, and when she sees the homeless man in the library, she is determined to interview him. A story of teenage rebellion and the harsh realities of the homeless and the Vietnam War.

Johnston, T. (2001). *Any small goodness: A novel of the barrio.* **New York: Scholastic/Blue Sky.** In the barrio of East Los Angeles, 11-year-old Arturo encounters some gang members who "just enjoy sending fear-ripples over people." Spanish expressions and numerous local references contribute to the rich setting and characters.

Lord, B. B. (1984). *In the Year of the Boar and Jackie Robinson.* **New York: Harper.** In 1947, a 10-year-old Chinese girl named Shirley comes to Brooklyn. She doesn't know English and has a difficult time making friends, but when she becomes friends with the toughest girl in the class, the other kids include her in their games.

Martin, A. M. (2002). *A corner of the universe.* **New York: Scholastic.** Almost-12-year-old Hattie Owen expects the summer of 1960 to be as comfortable and uneventful as others have been. She's looking forward to helping her mother run their boarding house with its eccentric adult boarders. When Adam commits suicide, she realizes that none of them had understood Adam as much as he needed them to. A Newbery Honor book.

Philbrick, R. (1993). *Freak the mighty.* **New York: Scholastic/Blue Sky Press.** Max and Kevin, two picked-on boys, combine their strengths to eliminate their weaknesses and take on the world and its bullies. Told in retrospect by Max, this is a poignant story of friendship and acceptance, with two extraordinary characters.

Rowling, J. K. (Series; years vary). *Harry Potter.* **New York: Scholastic.** The Harry Potter series is a study in resiliency, empathy, and tolerance, as an orphan boy and his friends fight for what they believe in, even when the odds are stacked against them.

Spinelli, J. (1996). *Crash.* **New York: Knopf.** Crash Coogan is a football player, completely confident, and the tormentor of Penn Webb, a friendly, small, pacifist Quaker. Crash's beloved grandfather comes to live with the family and suffers a disabling stroke, which leads to changes in Crash's lifestyle and values.

Strasser, T. (2000). *Give a boy a gun.* **New York: Simon & Schuster.** This chilling account of two boys who take their high school classmates hostage is told through interview-style snippets from the victims and the perpetrators. Footnotes about gun statistics and school violence appear throughout the story, and a list of additional resources is included.

Wilson, J. (2001). *Bad girls.* **New York: Delacorte.** Mandy White hates looking 8 years old when she's actually 10. And because of this, she's constantly being teased by the beautiful school bully, Kim. When Mandy forms a friendship with her new neighbor, a foster girl, they both learn from each other.

Resources for Teaching Public Spirit (Chapter 6)

PICTURE BOOKS

Clinton, C. (2018). *She persisted around the world: 13 women who changed history.* **New York: Penguin.** A book for everyone who has ever aimed high and was told to step down, and for everyone who raised their voice and was told to keep quiet. (Nonfiction)

Cooney, B. (1982). *Miss Rumphius.* **New York: Viking.** The fictional story of Miss Alice Rumphius, who traveled, had many adventures, and devotes herself to making the world more beautiful.

Fine, E. H., & Josephson, J. (2007). *Armando and the blue tarp school.* **New York: Lee & Low.** Armando longs to go school, but he needs to help his father pick through trash in the dump for things his family can use, recycle, or sell. This story is a testament to the pursuit of dreams and the power of one person to make a difference.

Krull, K. (2003). *Harvesting hope: The story of Cesar Chavez.* **Boston: Houghton Mifflin Harcourt.** The dramatic story of Chavez's 340-mile march to protest the working conditions of migrant farmworkers in California is central to this well-told picture book biography. Jane Addams Peace Award. (Nonfiction)

Krull, K. (2009). *The boy who invented TV: The story of Philo Farnsworth.* **New York: Knopf.** Covering Philo's life from his birth until the papers proclaimed him "a young genius," this inspiring picture book biography explores what imagination and diligence can accomplish. (Nonfiction)

Krull, K. (2019). *No truth without Ruth: The life of Ruth Bader Ginsburg.* **New York: HarperCollins.** Ruth Bader Ginsburg is one of the most respected women in the United States, but her recognition was hard won. This work is an empowering picture book biography about the second female justice of the Supreme Court. (Nonfiction)

Pearson, E. (2017). *Ordinary Mary's extraordinary deed.* **Layton, UT: Gibbs Smith.** What can happen when one ordinary child does one random good deed? It begins with Mary's simple act of kindness, which starts a chain reaction.

Rappaport, D. (2012). *Helen's big world: The life of Helen Keller.* **New York: Disney-Hyperion.** This picture book biography centers on one the world's most influential luminaries, whose vision for innovation and progress changed America, and the world, forever. (Nonfiction)

Ryan, P. M. (2002). *When Marian sang.* **New York: Scholastic.** Marian Anderson is best known for her historic concert on the steps of the Lincoln Memorial in 1939. This book highlights both the obstacles Anderson faced during her career and her amazing accomplishments. (Nonfiction)

Steig, W. (1986). *Brave Irene.* **New York: Farrar, Straus and Giroux.** The dressmaker isn't feeling well, so her daughter, plucky Irene, volunteers to get the gown to the palace in time for the ball, despite a tremendous storm.

Yousafzai, M. (2017). *Malala's magic pencil.* **New York: Little, Brown.** Malala made a wish for a magic pencil so she could make people happy, erase the smell of garbage, or sleep an extra hour, but as she grew older, she saw the world needed fixing in other ways. Malala Yousafzai won the 2014 Nobel Peace Prize. (Nonfiction)

CHAPTER BOOKS

Brimner, L. D. (2014). *Strike! The farm workers' fight for their rights.* **Honesdale, PA: Calkins Creek.** In 1965 in Delano, California, hundreds of Filipino field hands laid down their tools and refused to harvest vines laden with fruit. Their actions unleashed one of the most important agricultural strikes in U.S. history. Soon Cesar Chavez and his farm workers joined in on the fight. (Nonfiction)

Brimner, L. D. (2017). *Twelve days in May: Freedom Ride, 1961.* **Honesdale, PA: Calkins Creek.** On May 4, 1961, a group of 13 black and white civil rights activists launched the Freedom Ride to challenge segregation on buses and at bus terminal facilities. 2018 Robert F. Sibert Informational Book Award Winner. (Nonfiction)

Carmon, I., & Knizhnik, S. (2017). *Notorious RBG: The life and times of Ruth Bader Ginsburg* **(Young Readers Edition). New York: HarperCollins.** Supreme Court Justice Ginsburg's tireless fight for equality and women's rights not only has inspired great strides in the workforce, but has impacted the law of the land. (Nonfiction)

Davis, A. (2006). *The civically engaged reader: A diverse collection of short provocative readings on civic activity.* **Chicago: Great Books Foundation.** A collection of short readings from literature, philosophy, and criticism chosen to promote discussion and debate. Includes questions to guide dialogue.

Fadiman, A. (1997). *The spirit catches you and you fall down: A Hmong child, her doctors, and the collision of two cultures.* **New York: Farrar, Straus and Giroux.** This modern classic explores misguided Western medicine and a family who sees treatment and illness quite differently. (Nonfiction)

Fleischman, P. (1997). *Seedfolks.* **New York: Harper.** Stories told by different characters who live around Gibb Street in Cleveland, Ohio, describe how they transform an empty lot into a community garden and how the experience provides their own personal transformation.

French, S. T. (2011). *Operation Redwood.* **New York: Abrams.** A company owned by Julian's uncle is planning to cut down some of the oldest and last California redwood trees, and Julian and his friends are determined to stop it.

Hiaasen, C. (2002). *Hoot.* **New York: Knopf.** Roy joins an effort to stop construction of a pancake house, which would destroy a colony of owls. The construction foreman denies their existence, but Roy and his friends investigate and expose the truth. A Newbery Honor book.

Hoose, P. (2010). *Claudette Colvin: Twice toward justice.* **New York: Square Fish.** Nine months before Rosa Parks became famous by refusing to give up her seat on a bus, 15-year-old Claudette refused to give up hers. She was shunned by the community for her actions. "When it comes to justice, there is no easy way to get it. You can't sugarcoat it. You have to take a stand and say, 'this is not right.'" (Nonfiction)

Yousafzai, M., & McCormick, P. (2014). *I am Malala: How one girl stood up for education and changed the world* **(Young Readers Edition). New York: Little Brown.** Malala was only 10 years old when the Taliban took control of her region and said that women couldn't go to the market and girls couldn't go to school. This is the inspiring memoir of a Nobel Prize laureate who stood up for what she believes. (Nonfiction)

References

Adesope, O. O., Trevisan, D. A., & Sundararajan, N. (2017). Rethinking the use of tests: A meta-analysis of practice testing. *Review of Educational Research, 87*(3), 659–701. doi:10.3102/0034654316689306

Alexander, K. (2014). *The crossover.* New York: Houghton Mifflin Harcourt.

Andreae, G. (2012). *Giraffes can't dance.* New York: Scholastic.

Applegate, K. (2015). *The one and only Ivan.* New York: HarperCollins.

Argyle, M., & Lu, L. (1990). Happiness and social skills. *Personality and Individual Differences, 11*(12), 1255–1261.

Avi. (1990). *The true confessions of Charlotte Doyle.* New York: Orchard Books.

Avi. (1995). *Poppy.* New York: Orchard Books.

Bandura, A. (2001). Social cognitive theory: An agentic perspective. *Annual Review of Psychology, 52,* 1–26. doi:10.1146/annurev.psych.52.1.1

Beaty, A. (2016). *Ada Twist, scientist.* New York: Abrams.

Berman, S., Chaffee, S., & Sarmiento, J. (2018, March 12). *The practice base for how we learn: Supporting students' social, emotional, and academic development.* Washington, DC: Aspen Institute, National Commission on Social, Emotional, and Academic Development. Retrieved from https://assets.aspeninstitute.org/content/uploads/2018/01/CDE-consensus-statement-1-23-18-v26.pdf

Boelts, M. (2016). *A bike like Sergio's.* New York: Penguin Random House.

Boyle-Baise, M., & Zevin, J. (2013). *Young citizens of the world: Teaching elementary social studies through civic engagement.* New York: Routledge.

Brackett, M., & Frank, C. (2017, September 11). Four mindful back-to-school questions to build emotional intelligence. *Washington Post.* Retrieved from https://www.washingtonpost.com/news/parenting/wp/2017/09/11/a-mindful-start-to-the-school-year-four-back-to-school-questions-to-build-emotional-intelligence

Bray, W. (2014). Fostering perseverance: Inspiring students to be "doers of hard things." *Teaching Children Mathematics, 21*(1), 5–7. doi:10.5951/teacchilmath.21.1.0005

Bryk, A. S., Sebring, P., Allensworth, E., Luppescu, S., & Easton, J. Q. (2010). *Organizing schools for improvement: Lessons from Chicago.* Chicago: University of Chicago Press.

Burdick-Will, J. (2013). School violent crime and academic achievement in Chicago. *Sociology of Education, 86*(4), 343–361. doi:10.1177/0038040713494225

Byland, A. A. (2015, June). From "tough kids" to change agents. *Educational Leadership, 72*(9), 28–34. Retrieved from http://www.ascd.org/publications/educational-leadership/jun15/vol72/num09/From-%C2%A3Tough-Kids%C2%A3-to-Change-Agents.aspx

Callaghan, M. (1936). All the years of her life. In *Now that April's here and other stories* (pp. 9–16). New York: Random House.

Casey, B. J., Somerville, L. H., Gotlib, I. H., Ayduk, O., Franklin, N. T., Askren, M. K., . . . & Shoda, Y. (2011). Behavioral and neural correlates of delay of gratification 40 years later. *Proceedings of the National Academy of Sciences, 108*(36), 14998–15003. doi:10.1073/pnas.1108561108

Collaborative for Academic, Social, and Emotional Learning. (2005). *Safe and sound: An educational leader's guide to evidence-based social and emotional learning (SEL) programs.* Chicago: Author.

Collins, S. (2008). *The hunger games.* New York: Scholastic.

Compas, B. E., Jaser, S. S., Bettis, A. H., Watson, K. H., Gruhn, M. A., Dunbar, J. P., . . . & Thigpen, J. C. (2017). Coping, emotion regulation, and psychopathology in childhood and adolescence: A meta-analysis and narrative review. *Psychological Bulletin, 143*(9), 939–991. doi:10.1037/bul0000110

Costello, B., Wachtel, J., & Wachtel, T. (2009). *The restorative practices handbook for teachers, disciplinarians and administrators.* Bethlehem, PA: International Institute for Restorative Practices.

Cuddy, A. (2015). *Presence: Bringing your boldest self to your biggest challenges.* New York: Little, Brown.

Cuddy, A., Fiske, S., & Glick, P. (2007). The BIAS map: Behaviors from intergroup affect and stereotypes. *Journal of Personality and Social Psychology, 92*(4), 631–648. doi:10.1037/0022-3514.92.4.631

Cuddy, A. J. C., Schultz, A. J., & Fosse, N. E. (2018). *P*-curving a more comprehensive body of research on postural feedback reveals clear evidential value for power-posing effects: Reply to Simmons and Simonsohn. *Psychological Science, 29*(4), 656–666.

Danese, A., & McEwen, B. S. (2012). Adverse childhood experiences, allostasis, allostatic load, and age-related disease. *Physiology & Behavior, 106*(1), 29–39. doi:10.1016/j.physbeh.2011.08.019

Daniels, H. (2002). *Literature circles: Voice and choice in book clubs and reading groups* (2nd ed.). Portland, ME: Stenhouse.

Delpit, L. (2012). *"Multiplication is for white people": Raising expectations for other people's children.* New York: New Press.

Demi. (1997). *One grain of rice: A mathematical folktale.* New York: Scholastic.

Dendy, L., & Boring, M. (2005). *Guinea pig scientists: Bold self-experimenters in science and medicine.* New York: Holt.

Desliver, D. (2016, June 10). Turnout was high in the 2016 primary season, but just short of 2008 record. *Pew Research Center.* Retrieved from http://www.pewresearch.org/fact-tank/2016/06/10/turnout-was-high-in-the-2016-primary-season-but-just-short-of-2008-record/

DeWitt, P. (2018, January 4). 4 ways to get skeptics to embrace social-emotional learning: Educators must pay attention to students' well-being. *EdWeek.* Retrieved from https://www.edweek.org/ew/articles/2018/01/05/4-ways-to-get-skeptics-to-embrace.html

Duncan, G. J., Dowsett, C. J., Claessens, A., Magnuson, K., Huston, A. C., Klebanov, P., . . . & Japel, C. (2007). School readiness and later achievement. *Developmental Psychology, 43,* 1428–1446. doi:10.1037/0012-1649.43.6.1428

Dunlosky, J., & Rawson, K. (2012). Overconfidence produces underachievement: Inaccurate self evaluations undermine students' learning and retention. *Learning and Instruction, 22*(4), 271–280. doi:10.1016/j.learninstruc.2011.08.003

Durlak, J. A., Weissberg, R. P., Dymnicki, A. B., Taylor, R. D., & Schellinger, K. B. (2011). The impact of enhancing students' social and emotional learning: A meta-analysis of school-based universal interventions. *Child Development, 82*(1), 405–432. doi:10.1111/j.1467-8624.2010.01564.x

Durlak, J. A., Weissberg, R. P., & Pachan, M. (2010). A meta-analysis of after-school programs that seek to promote personal and social skills in children and adolescents. *American Journal of Community Psychology, 45*(3–4), 294–309. doi:10.1007/s10464-010-9300-6

Dweck, C. S. (2006). *Mindset: The new psychology of success.* New York: Ballantine.

Elias, M. J., Zins, J. E., Weissberg, R. P., Frey, K. S., Greenberg, M. T., Haynes, N. M., . . . Shriver, T. P. (1997). *Promoting social and emotional learning: Guidelines for educators.* Alexandria, VA: ASCD.

Farnam Street. (n.d.). Carol Dweck: A summary of the two mindsets and the power of believing that you can improve [blog post]. Retrieved from https://fs.blog/2015/03/carol-dweck-mindset/

Finnis, M. (2018, April 6). 33 ways to build better relationships. Retrieved from https://www.independentthinking.co.uk/blog/posts/2018/april/33-ways-to-build-better-relationships/

Fisher, D., & Frey, N. (2011). *The purposeful classroom: How to structure lessons with learning goals in mind.* Alexandria, VA: ASCD.

Fisher, D., & Frey, N. (2014, November). Speaking volumes. *Educational Leadership 72*(3), 18–23.

Fisher, D., Frey, N., & Pumpian, I. (2012). *How to create a culture of achievement in your school and classroom.* Alexandria, VA: ASCD.

Fisher, D., Frey, N., Quaglia, R. J., Smith, D., & Lande, L. L. (2017). *Engagement by design: Creating learning environments where students thrive.* Thousand Oaks, CA: Corwin.

Flake, S. (2007). *The skin I'm in.* New York: Hyperion.

Flegenheimer, C., Lugo-Candelas, C., Harvey, E., & McDermott, J. M. (2018). Neural processing of threat cues in young children with attention-deficit/hyperactivity symptoms. *Journal of Clinical Child & Adolescent Psychology, 47*(2), 336–344. doi:10.1080/15374416.2017.1286 593

Frey, N., Fisher, D., & Nelson, J. (2013). Todo tiene que ver con lo que se habla: It's all about the talk. *Phi Delta Kappan, 94*(6), 8–13. doi:10.1177/003172171309400603

Furr, R. M., & Funder, D. C. (1998). A multimodal analysis of personal negativity. *Journal of Personality and Social Psychology, 74*(6), 1580–1591.

Gerdes, K., Segal, E., Jackson, K., & Mullins, J. (2011). Teaching empathy: A framework rooted in social cognitive neuroscience and social justice. *Journal of Social Work Education, 47*(1), 109–131. doi:10.5175/JSWE.2011.200900085

Gergen, D. (2012, September 30). A candid conversation with Sandra Day O'Connor: "I can still make a difference." *Parade.* Retrieved from https://parade.com/125604/davidgergen/30-sandra-day-oconnor-i-can-make-a-difference/

Gordon, M. (2009). *Roots of empathy: Changing the world child by child.* New York: The Experiment.

Gordon, S. C., Dembo, M. H., & Hocevar, D. (2007). Do teachers' own learning behaviors influence their classroom goal orientation and control ideology? *Teaching and Teacher Education, 23*(1), 36–46. doi:10.1016/j.tate.2004.08.002

Hannah, S. T., Sweeney, P. J., & Lester, P. B. (2010). The courageous mind-set: A dynamic personality system approach to courage. In C. L. S. Pury & S. J. Lopez (Eds.), *The psychology of courage: Modern research on an ancient virtue* (pp. 125–148). Washington, DC: American Psychological Association.

Harrington, N. G., Giles, S. M., Hoyle, R. H., Feeney, G. J., & Yungbluth, S. C. (2001). Evaluation of the All Stars character education and problem behavior prevention program: Effects on mediator and outcome variables for middle school students. *Health Education & Behavior, 28*(5), 533–546. doi:10.1177/109019810102800502

Hattie, J. (2009). *Visible learning: A synthesis of over 800 meta-analyses relating to achievement.* New York: Routledge.

Hattie, J., & Timperley, H. (2007). The power of feedback. *Review of Educational Research, 77*(1), 81–112.

Hawkins, J. D., Smith, B. H., & Catalano, R. F. (2004). Social development and social and emotional learning. In J. E. Zins, R. P. Weissberg, M. C. Wang, & H. J. Walberg (Eds.), *Building academic success on social and emotional learning: What does the research say?* (pp. 135–150). New York: Teachers College Press.

Henderson, N. (2013, September). Havens of resilience. *Educational Leadership, 71*(1), 22–27.

Hinton, S. E. (1967). *The outsiders.* New York: Viking Press.

Hoffman, M. (1991). *Amazing Grace.* New York: Dial Books/Penguin.

House, B., & Tomasello, M. (2018). Modeling social norms increasingly influences costly sharing in middle childhood. *Journal of Experimental Child Psychology, 171,* 84–98. doi:10.1016/j.jecp.2017.12.014

Humphrey, N., Kalambouka, A., Wigelsworth, M., Lendrum, A., Deighton, J., & Wolpert, M. (2011). Measures of social and emotional skills for children and young people: A systematic review. *Educational and Psychological Measurement, 71*(4), 617–637. doi:10.1177/0013164410382896

Huntington, J. F. (2016). *The resiliency quiz.* Chevy Chase, MD: Huntington Resiliency Training. Retrieved from http://www.huntingtonresiliency.com/the-resiliency-quiz/

Jacobson, N., & Ross, G. (2012). *The hunger games* [motion picture]. United States: Lionsgate Films.

James-Ward, C., Fisher, D., Frey, N., & Lapp, D. (2013). *Using data to focus instructional improvement.* Alexandria, VA: ASCD.

Jiang, Y. J., Ma, L., & Gao, L. (2016). Assessing teachers' metacognition in teaching: The Teacher Metacognition Inventory. *Teaching and Teacher Education, 59,* 403–413. doi:10.1016/j.tate.2016.07.014

Johnston, P. H. (2004). *Choice words: How our language affects children's learning.* Portsmouth, NH: Stenhouse.

Jones, S., Bailey, R., Brush, K., & Kahn, J. (2018). *Preparing for effective SEL implementation.* Cambridge, MA: Harvard Graduate School of Education.

Jones, S., Brush, K., Bailey, K., Brion-Meisels, G., McIntyre, J., Kahn, J., . . . & Stickle, L. (2017). *Navigating SEL from the inside out. Looking inside & across 25 leading SEL programs: A practical resource for schools and OST providers (elementary school focus).* Cambridge, MA: Harvard Graduate School of Education and the Wallace Foundation. Retrieved from http://www.wallacefoundation.org/knowledge-center/Documents/Navigating-Social-and-Emotional-Learning-from-the-Inside-Out.pdf

Jordan, D., & Jordan, R. M. (2003). *Salt in his shoes: Michael Jordan in pursuit of a dream.* New York: Simon & Schuster.

Kackar-Cam, H., & Schmidt, J. (2014). Community-based service-learning as a context for youth autonomy, competence, and relatedness. *The High School Journal, 98*(1), 83–108. doi:10.1353/hsj.2014.0009

Kamkwamba, W., & Mealer, B. (2010). *The boy who harnessed the wind: Creating currents of electricity and hope.* New York: HarperCollins.

Katz, L., Sax, C., & Fisher, D. (2003). *Activities for a diverse classroom: Connecting students* (2nd ed.). Colorado Springs, CO: PEAK.

Kawashima-Ginsberg, K. (2012, December). *Summary of findings from the evaluation of iCivics' Drafting Board intervention* (CIRCLE Working Paper #76). Medford, MA: Tufts University, Center for Information & Research on Civic Learning & Engagement. Retrieved from http://www.civicyouth.org/wp-content/uploads/2012/12/WP_76_KawashimaGinsberg.pdf

Kidd, C., Palmeri, H., & Aslin, R. N. (2013). Rational snacking: Young children's decision-making on the marshmallow task is moderated by beliefs about environmental reliability. *Cognition, 126*(1), 109–114. doi:10.1016/j.cognition.2012.08.004

King, R. R., & Datu, J. A. (2017). Happy classes make happy students: Classmates' well-being predicts individual student well-being. *Journal of School Psychology, 65,* 116–128.

Kohlberg, L. (1963). The development of children's orientations toward a moral order: I. Sequence in the development of moral thought. *Vita Humana, 6*(1–2), 11–33.

Kristian, B. (2014, September 19). Nearly two-thirds of Americans can't name all three branches of the government. *The Week.* Retrieved from http://theweek.com/speedreads/445970/nearly-twothirds-americans-cant-name-all-three-branches-government

Kuypers, L. (2013). The zones of regulation: A framework to foster self-regulation. *Sensory Integration, 36*(4), 1–3.

Lamott, A. (1995). *Bird by bird: Some instruction on writing and life.* New York: Anchor.

LeCompte, K., Moore, B., & Blevins, B. (2011). The impact of iCivics on students' core civic knowledge. *Research in the Schools, 18*(2), 58–74.

Lee, D. S., Ybarra, O., Gonzalez, R., & Ellsworth, P. (2018). I-through-we: How supportive social relationships facilitate personal growth. *Personality & Social Psychology Bulletin, 44*(1), 37–48. doi:10.1177/0146167217730371

Levine, P., & Kawashima-Ginsberg, K. (2017, September 21). *The Republic is (still) at risk—And civics is part of the solution. A briefing paper for the Democracy at a Crossroads National Summit.* Retrieved from http://www.civxnow.org/documents/v1/SummitWhitePaper.pdf

Liberman, Z. L., & Shaw, A. (2017). Children use partial resource sharing as a cue to friendship. *Journal of Experimental Child Psychology, 159,* 96–109.

Lionni, L. (1996). *It's mine!* New York: Dragonfly Books.

Lithwick, D. (2018, February 28). They were trained for this moment. How the student activists of Marjory Stoneman Douglas High demonstrate the power of a comprehensive education. *Slate.* Retrieved from https://slate.com/news-and-politics/2018/02/the-student-activists-of-marjory-stoneman-douglas-high demonstrate-the-power-of-a-full-education.html

Lower, L. M., Newman, T. J., & Anderson-Butcher, D. (2017). Validity and reliability of the Teamwork Scale for Youth. *Research on Social Work Practice, 27*(6), 716–725. doi:10.1177/1049731515589614

Lowry, L. (1989). *Number the stars.* Boston: Houghton Mifflin Harcourt.

Macgowan, M. J., & Wong, S. E. (2017). Improving student confidence in using group work standards. *Research on Social Work Practice, 27*(4), 434–440. doi:10.1177/1049731515587557

Maclellan, E. (2014). How might teachers enable learner self-confidence? A review study. *Educational Review, 66*(1), 59–74. doi:10.1080/00131911.2013.768601

Maier, S., & Seligman, M. (1976). Learned helplessness: Theory and evidence. *Journal of Experimental Psychology: General, 105*(1), 3–46. doi:10.1037/0096-3445.105.1.3

Marinak, B. A., & Gambrell, L. B. (2016). *No more reading for junk: Best practices for motivating readers.* Portsmouth, NH: Heinemann.

Marsden, P. (1998). Memetics and social contagion: Two sides of the same coin? *Journal of Memetics: Evolutionary Models of Information Transmission, 2.* Retrieved from http://cfpm.org/jom-emit/1998/vol2/marsden_p.html

Marulis, L. M., Palincsar, A., Berhenke, A., & Whitebread, D. (2016). Assessing metacognitive knowledge in 3–5 year olds: The development of a metacognitive knowledge interview (McKI). *Metacognition and Learning, 11*(3), 339–368. doi:10.1007/s11409-016-9157-7

Mattis, J. S., Hammond, W. P., Grayman, N., Bonacci, M., Brennan, W., Cowie, S.A., . . . & So, S. (2009). The social production of altruism: Motivations for caring action in a low-income urban community. *American Journal of Community Psychology, 43*(1–2), 71–84. doi:10.1007/s10464-008-9217-5

Mayer, J., Salovey, P., & Caruso, D. (2000). Emotional intelligence as zeitgeist, as personality, and as a mental ability. In R. Bar-On & J. D. A. Parker (Eds.), *The handbook of emotional intelligence* (pp. 92–117). San Francisco: Jossey-Bass.

McConnell, C. (2011). *The essential questions handbook, grades 4–8.* New York: Scholastic.

Midgley, C. (Ed.). (2002). *Goals, goal structures, and patterns of adaptive learning.* Mahwah, NJ: Erlbaum.

Mikami, A. Y., Ruzek, E., Hafen, C., Gregory, A., & Allen, J. (2017). Perceptions of relatedness with classroom peers promote adolescents' behavioral engagement and achievement in secondary school. *Journal of Youth & Adolescence, 46*(11), 2341–2354.

Miller, L. (1989). Modeling awareness of feelings: A needed tool in the therapeutic communication workbox. *Perspectives in Psychiatric Care, 25*(2), 27–29. doi:10.1111/j.1744-6163.1989.tb00300.x

MindTools. (n.d.). Building self-confidence: Preparing yourself for success! Retrieved from https://www.mindtools.com/selfconf.html

Montgomery, S., Miller, W., Foss, P., Tallakson, D., & Howard, M. (2017). Banners for books: "Mighty-hearted" kindergartners take action through arts-based service learning. *Early Childhood Education Journal, 45*(1), 1–14. doi:10.1007/s10643-015-0765-7

Montroy, J. J., Bowles, R. P., Skibbe, L. E., McClelland, M. M., & Morrison, F. J. (2016). The development of self-regulation across early childhood. *Developmental Psychology, 52*(11), 1744–1762. doi:10.1037/dev0000159

Naragon-Gainey, K., McMahon, T. P., & Chacko, T. P. (2017). The structure of common emotion regulation strategies: A meta-analytic examination. *Psychological Bulletin, 143*(4), 384–427. doi:10.1037/bul0000093

National Geographic. (2008). *Every human has rights. A photographic declaration for kids.* New York: Penguin Random House.

National Youth Leadership Council. (2008). *K–12 service-learning standards for quality practice.* Saint Paul, MN: Author. Retrieved from https://nylc.org/wp-content/uploads/2015/10/standards_document_mar2015update.pdf

Nelson, A. E. (2009). *Social influence survey.* Retrieved from https://stca.org/documents/2016/6/Kidlead%20Social%20Influence%20Survey.pdf

Nelson, A. E. (2017). Mining student leadership gold. *Principal Leadership, 17*(7), 48–51.

Noddings, N. (2012). The caring relation in teaching. *Oxford Review of Education, 38*(6), 771–781. doi:10.1080/03054985.2012.745047

Norton, P. J., & Weiss, B. J. (2009). The role of courage on behavioral approach in a fear-eliciting situation: A proof-of-concept pilot study. *Journal of Anxiety Disorders, 23*(2), 212–217. doi:10.1016/j.janxdis.2008.07.002

Öhman, A., Flykt, A., & Esteves, F. (2001). Emotion drives attention: Detecting the snake in the grass. *Journal of Experimental Psychology, 130*(3), 466–478. doi:10.1037/0096-3445.130.3.466

O'Keefe, P. A., Ben-Eliyahu, A., & Linnenbrink-Garcia, L. (2013). Shaping achievement goal orientations in a mastery-structured environment and concomitant changes in related contingencies of self-worth. *Motivation and Emotion, 37*(1), 50–64. doi:10.1007/s11031-012-9293-6

Orwell, G. (1946). *Animal farm.* New York: Harcourt, Brace.

Palacio, R. J. (2012). *Wonder.* New York: Random House.

Palincsar, A. S., & Brown, A. L. (1984). Reciprocal teaching of comprehension-fostering and comprehension-monitoring activities. *Cognition and Instruction, 1*(2), 117–175. doi:10.1207/s1532690xci0102_1

Park, D., Tsukayama, E., Goodwin, G., Patrick, S., & Duckworth, A. (2017). A tripartite taxonomy of character: Evidence for intrapersonal, interpersonal, and intellectual competencies in children. *Contemporary Educational Psychology, 48,* 16–27. doi:10.1016/j.cedpsych.2016.08.001

Partnership for 21st Century Learning. (2015). The 4Cs research series. Retrieved from http://www.p21.org/our-work/4cs-research-series

Perkins, D. N., & Salomon, G. (1992). Transfer of learning. *International encyclopedia of education* (2nd ed.). Oxford: Pergamon.

Perkins-Gough, D., & Duckworth, A. (2013, September). The significance of GRIT. *Educational Leadership, 71*(1), 14–20.

Peterson, E., & Meissel, K. (2015). The effect of Cognitive Style Analysis (CSA) test on achievement: A meta-analytic review. *Learning and Individual Differences, 38,* 115–122. doi:10.1016/j.lindif.2015.01.011

Phelps, E. A. (2004). Human emotion and memory: Interactions of the amygdala and hippocampal complex. *Current Opinion in Neurobiology, 14*(2), 198–202. doi:10.1016/j.conb.2004.03.015

Pinker, S. (2012). *The better angels of our nature: Why violence has declined.* New York: Penguin.

Plutchik, R. (1997). The circumplex as a general model of the structure of emotions and personality. In R. Plutchik & H. R. Conte (Eds.), *Circumplex models of personality and emotions* (pp. 17–45). Washington, DC: American Psychological Association.

Posner, G. (1992). *Analyzing the curriculum* (2nd ed.). New York: McGraw-Hill.

Potter, L. A. (2016). Provoking student interest in civic responsibility with an 18th century diary entry. *Social Education, 80*(4), 224–226.

Ramirez, G., McDonough, I. M., & Ling, J. (2017). Classroom stress promotes motivated forgetting of mathematics knowledge. *Journal of Educational Psychology, 109*(6), 812–825. doi:10.1037/edu0000170

Rivera, J., & Docter, P. (2015). *Inside out* [motion picture]. United States: Walt Disney Pictures.

Republic [Def. 2]. (n.d.). In *Merriam-Webster online.* Retrieved from https://www.merriam-webster.com/dictionary/republic

Road Not Taken [computer software]. Kirkland, WA: Spry Fox.

Rosen, L. D. (2017). The distracted student mind—Enhancing its focus and attention. *Phi Delta Kappan, 99*(2), 8–14. doi:10.1177/0031721717734183

Ryan, P. M. (2000). *Esperanza rising.* New York: Scholastic.

Sapon-Shevin, M. (1998). *Because we can change the world: A practical guide to building cooperative, inclusive classroom communities.* Boston: Allyn & Bacon.

The Secretary's Commission on Achieving Necessary Skills. (1992). *Learning a living: A blueprint for high performance. A SCANS report for America 2000.* Washington, DC: U.S. Department of Labor. Retrieved from https://wdr.doleta.gov/scans/lal/lal.pdf

Shakur, T. (1999). *The rose that grew from concrete.* New York: MTV Books/Simon & Schuster.

Shannon, D. (2002). *David gets in trouble.* New York: Scholastic.

Shoda, Y., Mischel, W., & Peake, P. K. (1990). Predicting adolescent cognitive and self-regulatory competencies from preschool delay of gratification: Identifying diagnostic conditions. *Developmental Psychology, 26*(6), 978–986. doi:10.1037/0012-1649.26.6.978

Sisk, V. F., Burgoyne, A. P., Sun, J., Butler, J. L., & Macnamara, B. N. (2018). To what extent and under which circumstances are growth mind-sets important to academic achievement? Two meta-analyses. *Psychological Science, 29*(4), 549–571. doi:10.1177/0956797617739704

Smith, D., Fisher, D., & Frey, N. (2015). *Better than carrots or sticks: Restorative practices for positive classroom management.* Alexandria, VA: ASCD.

Smith, D., Frey, N. E., Pumpian, I., & Fisher, D. (2017). *Building equity: Policies and practices to empower all learners.* Alexandria, VA: ASCD.

Spinelli, J. (1990). *Maniac Magee.* New York: Little, Brown.

Spinelli, J. (1996). *Wringer.* New York: HarperCollins.

Sternberg, R. J. (1998). Metacognition, abilities, and developing expertise: What makes an expert student? *Instructional Science, 26*(1–2), 127–140. doi:10.1023/A:1003096215103

Stirin, K., Ganzach, Y., Pazy, A., & Eden, D. (2012). The effect of perceived advantage and disadvantage on performance: The role of external efficacy. *Applied Psychology, 61*(1), 81–96. doi:10.1111/j.1464-0597.2011.00457.x

Strom, B. S. (2016). Using service learning to teach *The Other Wes Moore*: The importance of teaching nonfiction as critical literacy. *English Journal, 105*(4), 37–42.

Talsma, K., Schüz, B., Schwarzer, R., & Norris, K. (2018). I believe, therefore I achieve (and vice versa): A meta-analytic cross-lagged panel analysis of self-efficacy and academic performance. *Learning and Individual Differences, 61,* 136–150. doi:10.1016/j.lindif.2017.11.015

Trollope, A. (2014). *Anthony Trollope: An autobiography and other writings.* (N. Shrimpton, Ed.). New York: Oxford University Press.

Ungar, M. (2008). Resilience across cultures. *British Journal of Social Work, 38*(2), 218–235. doi:10.1093/bjsw/bcl343

Ungar, M., Brown, M., Liebenberg, L., Othman, R., Kwong, W. M., Armstrong, M., & Gilgun, J. (2007). Unique pathways to resilience across cultures. *Adolescence, 42*(166), 287–310.

U.S. Department of Education, National Center for Education Statistics. (2015). *National Assessment of Educational Progress (NAEP), 2014 Civics assessments.* Retrieved from https://nces.ed.gov/nationsreportcard/civics/

United Nations. (1948, December 10). *The Universal Declaration of Human Rights.* Retrieved from http://www.un.org/en/universal-declaration-human-rights/

van der Linden, D. V., Pekaar, K. A., Bakker, A. B., Schermer, J. A., Vernon, P. A., Dunkel, C. S., & Petrides, K. V. (2017). Overlap between the general factor of personality and emotional intelligence: A meta-analysis. *Psychological Bulletin, 143*(1), 36–52. doi:10.1037/bul0000078

Vasquez, J. (1989). Contexts of learning for minority students. *The Educational Forum, 52*(3), 243–253. doi:10.1080/00131728809335490

Vogel, S., & Schwabe, L. (2016). Learning and memory under stress: Implications for the classroom. *NPJ Science of Learning, 1*, 1–10. doi:10.1038/npjscilearn.2016.11

Waters, E., & Sroufe, L. A. (1983). Social competence as a developmental construct. *Developmental Review, 3*(1), 79–97. doi:10.1016/0273-2297(83)90010-2

White, R. E., Prager, E. O., Schaefer, C., Kross, E., Duckworth, A., & Carlson, S. M. (2017). The "Batman effect": Improving perseverance in young children. *Child Development, 88*(5), 1563–1571. doi:10.1111/cdev.12695

Williams, V. B. (1982). *A chair for my mother.* New York: HarperCollins.

Wilson, D. B., Gottfredson, D. C., & Najaka, S. S. (2001). School-based prevention of problem behaviors: A meta-analysis. *Journal of Quantitative Criminology, 17*(3), 247–272. doi:10.1023/A:1011050217296

Zimmerman, B. J. (1989). A social cognitive view of self-regulated academic learning. *Journal of Educational Psychology, 81*(3), 329–339. doi:10.1037/0022-0663.81.3.329

Index

The letter *f* following a page number denotes a figure.

About the Authors

 **Nancy Frey** is a professor of educational leadership at San Diego State University and a teacher leader at Health Sciences High & Middle College. Before joining the university faculty, Frey was a special education teacher in the Broward County (Florida) Public Schools, where she taught students at the elementary and middle school levels. She later worked for the Florida Department of Education on a statewide project for supporting students with disabilities in a general education curriculum. Frey is a recipient of the Christa McAuliffe Award for Excellence in Teacher Education from the American Association of State Colleges and Universities and the Early Career Award from the Literacy Research Association. Her research interests include reading and literacy, assessment, intervention, and curriculum design. She has published many articles and books on literacy and instruction, including *Better Learning Through Structured Teaching* and *How to Reach the Hard to Teach*. She can be reached at nfrey@mail.sdsu.edu.

Douglas Fisher is a professor of educational leadership at San Diego State University and a teacher leader at Health Sciences High & Middle College. He is a member of the California Reading Hall of Fame and is the recipient of a Celebrate Literacy Award from the International Reading Association, the Farmer Award for Excellence in Writing from the National Council of Teachers of English, and a Christa McAuliffe Award for Excellence in Teacher Education from the American Association of State Colleges and Universities. Fisher has published numerous articles on improving student achievement, and his books include *The Purposeful Classroom, Enhancing RTI,* and *Intentional and Targeted Teaching*. He can be reached at dfisher@mail.sdsu.edu.

Dominique Smith is the chief of educational services and teacher support at Health Sciences High & Middle College, where he also serves as a culture builder and student advocate. He is the coauthor of *Better Than Carrots or Sticks: Restorative Practices for Positive Classroom Management* and *Building Equity: Policies and Practices to Empower All Learners*. Smith holds a master's degree in social work from the University of Southern California and an EdD in educational leadership from San Diego State University. He received the National School Safety Award from the School Safety Advocacy Council. He can be reached at dsmith@hshmc.org.

Related ASCD Resources: Social and Emotional Learning

At the time of publication, the following resources were available (ASCD stock numbers in parentheses):

PD Online® Courses
An Introduction to the Whole Child (#PD13OC009M)

Print Products
Better Than Carrots or Sticks: Restorative Practices for Positive Classroom Management by Dominique Smith, Douglas Fisher, and Nancy Frey (#116005)

Cultivating Habits of Mind (Quick Reference Guide) by Arthur L. Costa and Bena Kallick (#QRG117098)

The Formative Five: Fostering Grit, Empathy, and Other Success Skills Every Student Needs by Thomas R. Hoerr (#116043)

Integrating SEL into Everyday Instruction (Quick Reference Guide) by Nancy Frey, Dominique Smith, and Douglas Fisher (#QRG119030)

Relationships, Responsibility, and Regulation: Trauma-Invested Practices for Fostering Resilient Learning by Kristin Souers with Pete Hall (#119027)

Self-Regulated Learning for Academic Success: How do I help students manage their thoughts, behaviors, and emotions? (ASCD Arias) by Carrie Germeroth and Crystal Day-Hess (#SF114041)

Teaching to Strengths: Supporting Students Living with Trauma, Violence, and Chronic Stress by Debbie Zacarian, Lourdes Alvarez-Ortiz, and Judie Haynes (#117035)

What If? Building Students' Problem-Solving Skills Through Complex Challenges by Ronald Beghetto (#118009)

With the Whole Child in Mind: Insights from the Comer School Development Program by Linda Darling-Hammond, Channa M. Cook-Harvey, Lisa Flook, Madelyn Gardner, and Hanna Melnick (#119028)

For up-to-date information about ASCD resources, go to www.ascd.org. You can search the complete archives of *Educational Leadership* at www.ascd.org/el.

ASCD myTeachSource®
Download resources from a professional learning platform with hundreds of research-based best practices and tools for your classroom at http://myteachsource.ascd.org/

For more information, send an e-mail to member@ascd.org; call 1-800-933-2723 or 703-578-9600; send a fax to 703-575-5400; or write to Information Services, ASCD, 1703 N. Beauregard St., Alexandria, VA 22311-1714 USA.

WHOLE CHILD
TENETS

1 HEALTHY
Each student enters school healthy and learns about and practices a healthy lifestyle.

2 SAFE
Each student learns in an environment that is physically and emotionally safe for students and adults.

3 ENGAGED
Each student is actively engaged in learning and is connected to the school and broader community.

4 SUPPORTED
Each student has access to personalized learning and is supported by qualified, caring adults.

5 CHALLENGED
Each student is challenged academically and prepared for success in college or further study and for employment and participation in a global environment.

THE WHOLE CHILD

The ASCD Whole Child approach is an effort to transition from a focus on narrowly defined academic achievement to one that promotes the long-term development and success of all children. Through this approach, ASCD supports educators, families, community members, and policymakers as they move from a vision about educating the whole child to sustainable, collaborative actions.

All Learning is Social and Emotional relates to **all five** *tenets.*

For more about the ASCD Whole Child approach,
visit **www.ascd.org/wholechild.**

Become an ASCD member today!
Go to www.ascd.org/joinascd
or call toll-free: 800-933-ASCD (2723)

LEARN. TEACH. LEAD.